See Sam Run

A Mother's Story of Autism

by Peggy Heinkel-Wolfe

Number 2 in the Mayborn Literary Nonfiction Series

UNT
UPRESS

University of North Texas Press
Mayborn Graduate Institute of Journalism
Denton, Texas

10 9 8 7 6 5 4 3 2 1

Permissions:
University of North Texas Press
P.O. Box 311336
Denton, TX 76203-1336

The paper used in this book meets the minimum requirements of the American National Standard for Permanence of Paper for Printed Library Materials, z39.48.1984. Binding materials have been chosen for durability.

Library of Congress Cataloging-in-Publication Data

Heinkel-Wolfe, Peggy.
  See Sam run : a mother's story of autism / by Peggy Heinkel-Wolfe.
    p. cm. — (Mayborn literary nonfiction series ; no. 2)
  Includes bibliographical references.
  ISBN 978-1-57441-244-4 (cloth : alk. paper)
  1. Heinkel-Wolfe, Peggy. 2. Wolfe, Sam. 3. Parents of autistic children—Texas—Biography. 4. Autistic children—Texas—Biography. I. Title.
  RJ506.A9H43 2008
  616.85'8820092—dc22
  [B]
                            2007048882

See Sam Run is
Number 2 in the Mayborn Literary Nonfiction Series

About this book
All the names in this book are the true names of people who have touched our lives. In addition to his Senior Scrapbook essay in the epilogue, Sam wrote the photo captions.

Text design by Carol Sawyer of Rose Design

To Mark,
with all my heart

CONTENTS

Year One

Year Two

Year Three

Year Four

Epilogue

Senior Scrapbook

Appendix 1

Appendix 2

The Beginning

SOME GIRLS DREAM OF BECOMING A MOM, but I wasn't one of them. I wanted to play the piano ever since I was six years old and heard my Aunt Helen play Beethoven's *Moonlight Sonata*.

I was nine when I started class piano lessons. In the beginning, I practiced at home on a cardboard keyboard my teacher gave me. I imagined a sound like Helen made. Dad eventually brought home a turn-of-the-century "upright grand" piano—a pizza-parlor cast-off covered in deep blue paint. When I first pressed down on the ebony and ivory keys, the sound I made resonated all the way through my bones.

That same year, one of my teachers at Byron Kilbourn Elementary School decided I was gifted. Had I attended fifth grade at Milwaukee's magnet school for gifted children, there would have been accelerated math, special study projects, even violin lessons, to go along with class piano I'd just started.

We visited the magnet school, but my parents wanted to think it over before enrolling me. Dad was attending Marquette University's School of Dentistry and we had only one car, a green Chevy Parkwood station wagon. I would have to ride a city bus every day to get to the new school.

Before Dad started dental school, he was a research biologist at the University of Wisconsin in Madison. I attended kindergarten at a well-appointed, private Catholic school near our home when I was four years old.

When we moved, I watched Dad make the first payment for our apartment in a public housing project on Milwaukee's west side with a one hundred dollar bill. I'd never seen one before. Mom and Dad had little to spend after that. Every time we drove by the Chocolate Shoppe, I hoped we'd stop to get ice cream cones. I liked Blue Moon flavor best. I dared to ask for an ice cream only once, but Mom and Dad said no.

The teachers at Byron Kilbourn Elementary struggled mightily to serve us kids from Westlawn, often breaking up fights during recess and waiting in empty classrooms on parent-teacher conference day. Mom told us we couldn't play on the neighborhood jungle gym because it was usually covered in broken glass. One night, we nearly had a riot in our neighborhood when a goodwill concert for interracial understanding disintegrated into a shouting match over the Vietnam War. As police descended on the angry gathering, Dad grabbed my hand. Carrying my little sisters, both he and Mom hustled us back to the apartment. Their silence was haunting.

On the way to the magnet school, that city bus would have taken me through even rougher neighborhoods. Fearing for my safety—and knowing we were moving soon after Dad graduated—my parents refused to enroll me.

The summer of 1971, before I turned eleven, we moved up north to a small town where Dad started his practice. New London was surrounded by hog and dairy farms. Some of my classmates helped with the milking each morning, stepping off the school bus with manure still stuck to their work boots. Others lived in town, like we did, and walked to school. New London was filled with families who'd known each other for generations. I didn't fit in. A classmate flirted with me on the way home from school once, but I didn't understand. Even though he was a head taller than me, I tackled him in a snowdrift and pummeled his face and belly with my fists. The other kids teased him. They laughed at me even more.

New Londoners sorted teenagers into good and bad. I was on my way to achieving the labels I didn't want—a bad girl, for being mouthy and streetwise, and a fat girl, simply because I was growing up. I withdrew to my piano, skimming through my lesson material so I could explore harmonies I found soothing or interesting, and improvising on them for hours.

Dad's dental practice grew fast. He moved out of his windowless downtown second-floor space next to the Wolf River and into a new building uptown. I liked the building's many picture windows overlooking the Embarrass River, its bed wild with maple trees and trillium. Dad paid me to clean the new office every Sunday to help save money for college.

He also junked the station wagon since the floorboards had rusted so much the taillights flickered. For fun, he test-drove a Mercedes-Benz, and then he bought that shiny, new maroon sedan on the spot.

Mom and Dad were strict with me and my sisters. I wasn't allowed to go to school dances or out-of-town games. I defied them once in the eighth grade and rode the school bus three miles to Hortonville to watch a junior varsity basketball game. The game had just started when Dad showed up in the doorway at the Hortonville High School gym. My friends noted his arrival with pointed fingers, saying, "Peggy, isn't that your dad?" Overwhelmed with embarrassment, I left the stands without making a scene.

In high school, I tried to be one of the good kids. I didn't get drunk, drugged out, or pregnant. I earned straight As, but my achievements didn't seem to matter. I always felt I wasn't good enough. In driver's education, I passed parallel parking on the first try, but Mom and Dad told me I wouldn't be allowed to get my license until I left for college.

My junior-high girlfriends shut me out of their circle in high school. I never found out why. Desperate for acceptance, I developed an eating disorder, well before magazines were describing the problem. I didn't have a word for mine. I drank broth for lunch during the school days and soaked up compliments from new friends about how slim I looked. But by night, my starving body rebelled. I ate and ate, and purged it all, starting the cycle over again. On a good day, I succumbed only once, but on a bad day, three or four times—rotting my teeth and popping blood vessels in my eyes.

By now, Dad worked long days. He golfed on Thursday afternoons and Saturdays. If he noticed the change in me, he didn't act on it. Mom oversaw endless renovations to the 125-year-old farmhouse we lived in and took to hippie things, like making pottery and back-to-the-earth cooking. If she noticed, she didn't act either.

My class of '78 graduation photo, taken on a sunny day beneath a beautiful birch tree, failed to hide my cloudy eyes and sallow skin tone. No one saw what I'd become, and I couldn't bear to look anymore.

My disease had become a gurge the summer before my senior year. One Saturday morning, when Dad was golfing and Mom was busy with my younger sisters, I woke up late, still reeling from a bad fight the night before with my boyfriend. I locked myself in the upstairs bathroom and surrendered, trying to swallow as many aspirin as I could. It was the most powerful drug my cautious parents kept in the house.

I didn't write a note, but wanted to say goodbye to someone, so I called my best friend and told her what I did. She called back and told Mom. As they wheeled me away, I saw through my own foggy vision Mom struggling to focus as she counted the remaining pills in that 500-count jar. I dutifully threw up the pills in the emergency room, just like I did my food at home.

I slept the first day or two. I didn't want to be awake, and thinking. On her shift, one of the night nurses stayed with me much longer than she had to during the wee hours. She rubbed my back and told me I was too young and pretty to be so sad.

After a few days, the hospital dispatched a psychiatrist to my room. He pulled a chair up next to my bed and slowly ran his index finger up and down the bed rail, asking me questions in a gentle voice. Our conversation drifted. I didn't have a vocabulary for my disease. After an hour, he said he wanted me to see him again after I got out of the hospital. I told Mom I didn't see the point. She didn't argue with me.

Later, Dr. Schmallenberg came. He wasn't my regular physician. He was golfing with Dad when I was rushed to the hospital. Dr. Schmallenberg sat on the edge of my bed while he studied my chart. He talked matter-of-factly about my body being slow in removing the toxins. My levels were troublesomely high, he said. I would have to stay several more days.

Mom and Dad agreed to keep my suicide attempt quiet. My boyfriend, bound for Air Force boot camp, never knew. But my attempt hurt Dad so much that he couldn't bear to visit me at New London Community Hospital for several days, until Mom gave him an ultimatum.

Help finally arrived via my high school guidance counselor. A bearded angel in plaid flannel shirts, he came every evening. He kept his chair against the wall at the foot of my bed, where rays of summer sunlight stretched just out of reach. I still didn't have the vocabulary, but he asked me better questions.

Every time I saw him step out of the counselor's office into the hallway between classes my senior year, our eyes met. I remembered that lingering summer sun outside my hospital window, coming to believe in the strong person he said I was. Another year went by, however, before I learned the name of what had nearly killed me.

Naming my monster helped me beat it in college, although it took my entire freshman year at the North Texas State University School of Music in Denton, Texas. I took one day at a time, first teaching myself to swim freestyle. I swam lap after lap until I was too tired to count them anymore. I went back home for summer break. Even though I swam in the city pool every day, I started to binge once a week or so. Terrified of a relapse, I would wait years to go home again.

Back in Denton the next fall, I swam in the morning and filled the rest of my day with my studies, rehearsals, and music practice. If I ate too much one day, I wouldn't torture myself to get rid of it. I told myself that my stomach, my throat, my teeth, my eyes, and my heart deserved a normal life, even if my head couldn't bear it.

Beating bulimia is a lot different than quitting drugs or alcohol. I still have to eat every day. It can't be all or nothing.

While in college, I eventually abandoned the piano for the euphonium, an instrument I'd started playing in high school so I could join the band. Even with its gorgeous sound, the euphonium had earned itself an odd place in the music world. Yet playing its characteristic parts—soaring countermelodies and sturdy inner harmonies—suited me. I practiced until my friend Dan, another euphonium student who worked as the building monitor, locked up at midnight. We walked home together, usually talking about music the whole way.

I followed my muse for nearly ten years, from Texas to New York and Japan, making several lifelong friends and performing wherever I could. During a fellowship in Tokyo, stories about me appeared in national music magazines. I didn't realize I had become a celebrity in Japan because I couldn't read the *kanji*. I was the first American to play in the rank and file of the Tokyo Kosei Wind Orchestra, the best group of its kind in the world, but I didn't know it until a longtime member of the group told me after the concert. As I turned in my music and packed up my instrument backstage, I basked in the glow as all the musicians exchanged a traditional, singsong farewell.

Otsuskarasamadeshita.

My friend Kaoru told me that this greeting rolled up "good job," "good night," and "congratulations" all in one. He also said it meant, more strictly translated, "I suppose you are Mr. Tired."

I wanted to stay in Japan with my creative friends, who staged concerts like an in-costume, all-euphonium rendition of *West Side Story*, and shamelessly sold tickets until the house was standing room only. But I had to go back. Within a year, I moved to California. An old college friend had become the new love in my life. The move also promised interesting career opportunities. Music was keeping me whole and happy.

Until one April afternoon.

"I'm calling about my pregnancy test," I told the nurse who answered the clinic phone.

"Could I have your record number, please?" she replied.

I read off the number.

"Your results were positive."

"Oh, okay." I realized how much I lacked rehearsal for this moment.

"You should call soon to schedule a prenatal appointment. You can discuss your options with the doctor at your first visit," she said.

I was afraid my fiancé, Mark, would be upset. Our wedding was still several weeks away. But he smiled this funny smile I'd never seen before, although by then, we'd dated on and off for five years, and been good friends even longer.

For several days we tried to talk about my pregnancy and couldn't. On one of the occasional Friday nights that Mark had off—the Sacramento Symphony concert had no tuba part that night—we stretched out over the bed, watching the late day sun through the shade screens and mulberry trees covered with bagworms, and we surrendered the idea that we were supposed to choose. We could make this work.

About ten weeks into my pregnancy, I made another phone call.

"Hi, Mom. It's me." I imagined my voice traveling east to Colorado, along telephone lines over two mountain ranges.

"Hi, you."

"I need your advice." *I've become just as economical a speaker as Dad*, I thought.

"What about?"

"First, I'm pregnant. But I'm also spotting."

"Oh my." I heard her take a breath. I wondered whether she was considering what she would say next. "Is it brown or bright red?"

"Brown."

"A little spotting isn't all that uncommon," she said. "You may be okay. But if you start bleeding, you'd better go in to see the doctor and get checked."

"Okay. I'm sorry to give you the news this way," I said.

"It's still happy news."

She paused.

"It's just that when I miscarried, that's how it started."

She paused again. I had been sixteen and clearly remembered what happened to her.

"Or it may be nothing. Just stay off your feet for a while."

That evening, I lay curled up on top of towels that I'd set on the bathroom floor, cramping and bleeding. A doctor in the emergency room had sent me home a few hours earlier, telling me that there was nothing they could do. I had to wait it out. Each time I got up from the tile floor to sit on the toilet, a fresh rush of blood flowed and frightened me.

Although I was ambivalent about being pregnant, I still wanted to control my body. I tried to visualize making the cramping and bleeding stop, but I couldn't come up with anything. I tried talking to myself. I tried talking to the baby. I heard Mark talking to someone on the phone downstairs. It was probably Mom again. I couldn't hear his words, but I knew by Mark's tone that he'd surrendered.

Finally, I fell asleep on the bathroom floor. Mark carried me to bed. When I woke up the next morning, the symptoms subsided. By day's end, the cramping and bleeding stopped altogether.

A month later, we got married in the carefree ceremony we'd wanted, standing barefoot on a black sand beach as the sun went down over the big island of Hawaii. As spring rolled into summer, my calendar filled up with doctor appointments. I yielded some of my practice time to reading a few books about pregnancy and baby care. I most enjoyed Lennart Nilsson's books chronicling a baby's growth in golden photographs. In the early months, my baby fluttered like the prehistoric fish he resembled. I was six months along before my belly started to show. I found it easy to continue keeping fit by swimming in the small pool adjacent to our townhouse.

In the fall, I signed Mark and myself up for a birthing class. The moms-to-be turned in a daily record of meals and snacks each week, adding up the grams of protein to make sure we met our daily requirements.

I also applied for a new job as the part-time director of a small arts council, in neighboring El Dorado County. The council's board of directors held interviews the same night as our last birthing class. *Just as well*, I thought. Maybe the other moms-to-be would feel ready for their babies after our little graduation ceremony. But I was beginning to wonder whether I would ever feel ready.

As I set up the baby's things in the corner of our second bedroom, already filled with instruments, a filing cabinet stuffed with sheet music, and one wall lined with bookshelves, I tried to sort through my ambivalence. I wasn't worried about either of us being good and loving caregivers. But we worked an unconventional schedule. I couldn't see how to fit a baby into it. I had already canceled one overseas trip. I feared most that having a baby would make my world small again.

I got the arts council job, and drove the forty-minute commute to a Placerville office several times a week until the organization relocated to a tiny historic house inside Coloma's Gold Discovery Park, deep in the Sierra foothills. The art gallery took up most of the space inside the little house. A co-worker and I shared an ancient oak desk squeezed in the back and several metal storage shelves in the restroom.

The gallery was quiet, and often cold, especially after the winter rains arrived. Northern California rains feed on giant, low-pressure systems parked over the Pacific. Back in Sacramento, the clouds sometimes come down to earth and sit. When I would walk around our neighborhood, familiar places would jump out of the fog and surprise me. People in the valley call it tule fog. The winter fog and rains vanish in March. The emerald green hills between Sacramento and Coloma roast golden brown. The weather, not the Gold Rush, had earned California its nickname, "The Golden State." Rain in Sacramento is all or nothing.

For what would be my last pregnancy checkup, we were out driving in another foggy rain, stuck in the Watt Avenue northbound queue at Fair Oaks Boulevard. Traffic had backed up all the way to the bridge over the American River. Mark moved the windshield wipers to the intermittent setting in order to match the pace of the misting rain. I shifted my weight from my left side to my right, fumbling with the seat belt across my belly. I couldn't sit up straight because the baby's head shifted down into my pelvis and pinched me. It was hard to tell where the strange pain came from, since everything was so smashed together. The baby was due December 7. It wouldn't be long now.

Our new Subaru four-door sedan idled smoothly as the wipers waved up and down, and paused before whisking the rain off again.

"Do you hear that?" I asked.

"What?" Mark said.

"In the wipers. That high-pitched grinding sound."

"Um, no," he replied. Up, down, pause. Up, down.

"I can't believe you can't hear that. Please, just turn them off," I begged.

I wondered why I was so sensitive to the sound and he wasn't, since he had perfect pitch.

Mark obliged. The light at Fair Oaks changed from red to green, and we crept forward a few more car lengths as the rain smoothed into a blanket over the windshield.

A few nights later, I woke up in wet, warm bed sheets. I thought I'd had an accident, but then I realized the sheets were soaked and growing wetter by the minute.

"Oh my god, Mark, I think my water broke," I said, grabbing his arm.

"Okay, I'm up, I'm up," he mumbled.

"Mark, my water broke," I repeated.

"We'd better go," he said, rolling out of bed. He stood up and squinted at the clock. "This is a few days early. What time is it?"

"It's three o'clock." I didn't have to look at the clock to know.

During the pregnancy, I had been able to tell the precise time without looking at the clock. In addition to being sensitive to certain sounds, I also became such a picky eater that Mark had learned to wait until I got home from work before he made us dinner. One night, he observed something about my requests that I hadn't.

"I've finally figured this out. You've got to have fresh, and never any old, food. No crackers, yogurt, stinky cheese, stuff like that," he had said, making me laugh.

I never read "You'll be overly sensitive to sound" or "You'll develop an innate sense of time" in any of my pregnancy books. A few said that pregnant women sometimes developed strange tastes, and some researchers linked that to the baby's nutritional needs. But I didn't believe anyone ever went out at night into the rain and fog for ice cream and pickles. Besides, pickles are old food.

6:12 a.m., 6 lbs. 15 oz.

Mark covered his nose with his hand and described for me what he saw as Sam was coming out.

"You know, when his head was . . . well, the doctor told the nurse that he was coming out sunny-side up. So I looked down. Even though I couldn't see Sam's nose yet, his eyes were wide open, and they were going from side to side. Like this." With his hand, he flattened his own nose right below the bridge, at the same spot where he'd stabbed himself with a pencil as a second grader. The injury left a little blue pencil dot that never faded. He moved his dark blue eyes rapidly from one side to the other. I smiled.

"It was amazing. He was so curious already. You should've seen him," he finished breathlessly.

I was too busy pushing to get in on any of that fun, I thought. *Where did Mark get this new burst of energy?* I was exhausted. Sam was fine, but the nurses had whisked him away soon after he was born. I was so tired that I didn't care.

"I'm going to go see him one more time before I go," Mark said. He leaned over and kissed me on the forehead. He wanted to go home and take a nap since he still had to play a concert that night. As he left, the nurse on duty seized the moment.

"Mrs. Wolfe, let's try one more time at the toilet," she said.

The nurse helped me stumble out of bed toward the bathroom door. As I sat down, I started thinking about the books that I had read. The books had said that babies come when they want to, but today I was learning that doctors have deadlines.

"I am so very upset and frustrated."

After my water broke, I walked for twelve hours to get labor going. Without any regular contractions, the doctor prescribed hormones to induce labor. Six or seven hours went by without much progress, and I was drained. One of the nurses had the hormone dosage increased and a muscle relaxant added. After that, I slept right through some contractions. I liked that. About three thirty in the morning, twenty-four hours after my water broke, time ran out and infection was a risk, the nurse explained to me. I'd signed consent papers for a C-section. But before they could begin, I managed to push my baby out on my own.

I turned off the warm water streaming over my left hand and began wondering where the recovery room nurse had gone. I was too swollen to go. Time was running out on me again. I tried to figure out when the doctor had done the episiotomy for the birth, but couldn't. The stitches hurt now. I couldn't remember whether the glossy pregnancy books had told me that I would vomit, or anything about deadlines for a postpartum pee.

The nurse came back a few minutes later. "No luck, huh? We'd better hook you up," she said, looking down at me. I surrendered to the catheter and, at last, to a long sleep.

I woke up later in a maternity room with three women in the other beds. Beyond the privacy curtains, I saw a little daylight behind the clouds in the narrow windows. I had no idea what time it was.

"Where's my baby?" I asked the nurse arriving a few minutes after I woke.

"In the nursery," she said.

"Can I see him?"

"Well, the rules are, you have to be well enough to get up and bring in your baby yourself," she said. She studied me. I hadn't seen myself in a mirror, but given how I felt, I knew I had to look pretty beat-up. "I suppose I could go get him for you this first time."

She pointed to the catheter bag as she left the room.

"Oh, as that gets full, you can go empty it yourself in the bathroom across the hall," she told me.

I glanced at the half-full bag and stared out the window again. *What's today?* I wondered. *Oh, yes, Mom and Dad are coming tomorrow.* They planned on arriving two days before Sam, but he had his own schedule.

The nurse returned, rolling a small cart that looked like a cupboard. A clear-sided bassinet sat on top. Sam was swaddled inside, tucked under a soft white cotton blanket. A blue knit cap covered his head.

"Do you want to try to nurse him?" she asked.

"I do." I reached into the bassinet and lifted him up. He wiggled and started to whine.

"Hi, Sam, it's me," I cooed. He calmed a bit at the sound of my voice.

Mark and I took our time choosing a name before Sam was born. We wanted something strong and dignified that would tie him to his extended family. I liked the sound of Samuel. Mark told me that it was his grandfather's name. I liked it even more when I researched its meaning: "wise one."

I unwrapped Sam's swaddling blanket. He smelled like unbaked cookies. His skin was wrinkled, yet tender, and the afterbirth layer was peeling away from his miniature knuckles and fingernails. His hair felt like downy peach fuzz and it was black, like Mark's.

I thought of the many people, known and unknown to me, who had asked "Do you want a boy or girl?" and to whom I had answered, "I just want ten fingers and ten toes."

As I lifted the side of my gown, I looked down and saw that several pads underneath me were soaked with blood. I wondered where they came from and why I didn't realize, before now, that they were there. Sam latched on. I felt a contraction. More blood rushed out. *It's a mess*, I thought. He sucked for a while. After a few minutes, I was too taxed to sit up. I shifted Sam over to my side and lay down. My milk hadn't come in yet, but Sam kept sucking until we both drifted back to sleep.

Robin came to visit before Mark returned that afternoon. I hardly knew her. She played flute in the orchestra and desperately wanted a baby, but her husband was balking. Or so Mark had told me. He told me that she might visit us in the hospital and I told him that I didn't mind.

Sam enchanted Robin. I watched her as she held him and cooed at him, wondering where her motherly feelings came from. At one point, my bed covers shifted. Robin saw one of my blood-soaked pads. She looked shocked. I hustled the covers back in place.

After Robin left, Mark came back. He told me that he'd napped, too, and gone into the symphony office to do a little paperwork afterward. He had accepted the orchestra's part-time personnel job, as I had done with the arts council, for the medical benefits and to make some extra money.

He brought out the camera and asked to take some pictures. I hadn't let him take any when Sam was being born, because I thought the images would frighten people, including me. Even now, my curly hair was matted, looking black instead of brown. I was bloated with saline solution. The freakishly puffy circles under my eyes looked like a pair of shiners. What was he thinking?

"Just one or two?" Mark said. "Otherwise we won't have any, except that canned baby picture that the hospital takes."

I acquiesced, knowing that no matter how gently he saw me, the photos would capture something we didn't want to remember. After they came back from the lab, he would see that I was right. We would keep those snapshots hidden, but Mark's mother stumbled upon them one day. Her gasp spoke volumes. I promptly threw them away.

Mark left for home to get dressed for the concert, and came back to the hospital one more time, after the concert was over, wearing his white tie and tails. I watched him while he visited with the nurses. He stood with his heels together, chest held high, a head taller than all but one of them. His posture reminded me of our college days, when we first became friends. He was a senior and I was a freshman. As the drum major of the marching band, he'd held himself that way back then, too. Now, his eyes looked watery and his wavy hair needed more than a finger-combing to look right.

Mark told me his back was hurting. During labor, we discovered that if he pushed his fist into the small of my back, the counterpressure gave me relief from the contractions that concentrated there. Unfortunately, I needed that counterpressure for hours, and he had to hold onto my gurney at the same time, lest it roll away.

"How about we ask Raeanne for a massage for you as a baby present?" I asked. Raeanne played violin in the orchestra and gave massages to make extra money.

"I can stay with Sam for a little while here, and wheel him back into the nursery when I leave, if you want to take a shower," he said.

I kissed him and picked up my loofah, shampoo, towel, and catheter stand, and wheeled myself slowly across the hall to the shower room.

The room was lined with small honey-colored tiles with a sitting place built into the wall. I turned on the faucet and watched the water bubble and swirl down the drain in the middle of the floor. The shower reminded me of a public bath in Japan that I'd had all to myself, since everyone else was soaking in the renowned, spring-fed baths outside. There, the amber tiles of the indoor bath gently descended under the water like a beach face. Steam rose and clung to the tiled walls and ceiling. Mozart piano sonatas unfolded over the sound system as a warm light glowed from a sculpture in the middle of the pool.

Pay attention, I told myself. *Life is going to be different now.* I took the massaging shower head from its holder, washing the sweat from my hair and the trauma from my skin. I dried off and pulled on a fresh gown. I went to get Sam from the nursery.

Sam and I would sleep together as often as I could claim him from the nursery. He seemed agitated, arching his back when I held him. Seeing that, one nurse suggested keeping him swaddled inside his receiving blanket as much as possible to help him feel safe. If I put him on my chest, the sound of my heartbeat calmed him, too.

Grandparents

Although Sam was my first baby, he wasn't Mom and Dad's first grandbaby. I had watched them help my younger sister, Chris, when her son, Ronnie, was born three years before. I asked them to come help us. I promised them we would all have plenty of fun together, too.

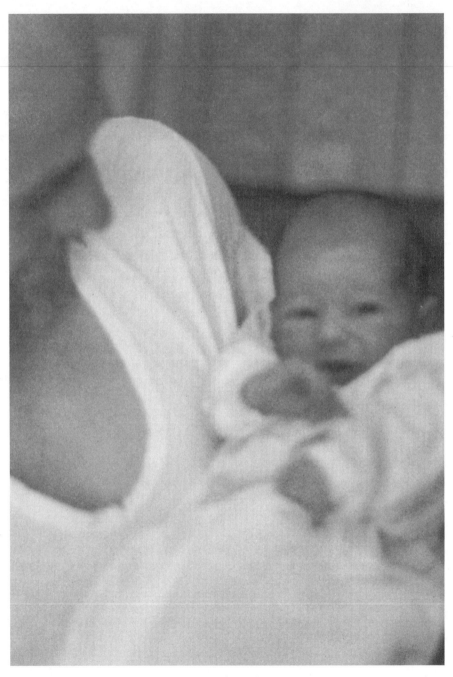

"I am sleepy."

The moment Mom and Dad arrived, they got to work shampooing the mini-shag carpets ("He'll be crawling before you know it") and cleaning out the kitchen cupboards ("You'll want the pots and pans where he can have his own fun while you're cooking").

The four of us passed Sam from one set of arms to another. During the day, he barely slept in the crib that Mark and I had refurbished for him. Sam also spent most nights sleeping on Mark's chest.

I hadn't anticipated how tired and disoriented I would feel following Sam's birth. I thought at twenty-seven I was young enough to bounce back quickly. I was wrong. I wasn't much company for Mom and Dad. We spent most of their visit flopped down inside our townhouse. One afternoon, I agreed to tour the newly renovated capitol building, but I became so exhausted from the tour that, at one point, I slid down the back wall of the elevator and sat on the floor while Sam cried—the sound muffled by the flannel-lined, corduroy front pack I carried him in.

One man heard Sam's cry and said it sounded like music. I thought he was crazy.

Mark entertained Mom and Dad one night by taking them along to an orchestra concert. Dad wore his western-trimmed sport coat and bolo tie and Mom wore a gray flannel sheath she had sewn. I stayed home in my cotton sweats while Sam cried uncontrollably, another night in a growing chain of long, restless evenings with my restless newborn.

Sam was a week old, but we weren't becoming more comfortable with each other. He seemed to grow unhappier each day. Often, he didn't fall asleep after a breastfeeding. Instead, he would cry for an hour or two, until he was hungry again. I tried Mom's suggestion to nurse him every ten minutes or so.

But he wasn't hungry, and offering only seemed to make him more frustrated.

When Sam had one of his crying jags, Mark put up a cheerful veneer. Maybe he hoped his happy face would be contagious. But Sam kept crying, and I couldn't fake it.

Dad became both annoyed and concerned, which always unnerved me. I never knew which emotion to respond to first. Now, because I also felt that I was not getting the hang of this baby thing, Dad's demeanor bothered me even more. When Sam cried, he needed to be nursed, changed, washed, and coaxed back to sleep. Before I could finish washing and changing myself, the cycle of caring for him started all over again.

On one of the last nights of Mom and Dad's visit, after a rushed trip to the grocery store because it took all day to get ready, I wondered out loud how I was going to care for Sam after my parents were gone. It's not that I expect their help all the time, I told Mark. But Dad planned on selling his practice in Colorado and going to work for a dental clinic in Saudi Arabia. With Mom and Dad out of the country, I couldn't think of anyone to call when we had a baby-care question. Mark told me I shouldn't worry. We could figure it out ourselves.

Years later, Mom would confess to me that Dad knew what Sam's faraway eyes and fussiness meant. He had even given it a word. But Mom didn't want to hear it and chastised Dad. How could he tell Mark and me such a thing so soon after Sam was born? So the word was never uttered around the two of us. Dad's dead-on diagnosis slipped away, silent and forgotten.

First Doctor Visit

"Your son has gained a pound and a half since he was born," the clinic pediatrician said. "That's pretty good. We usually look for babies to recover their birth weight by their two-week checkup. Are you breastfeeding?"

"We are," I replied.

The nurse asked me to remove Sam's diaper for his weigh-in. As I answered the doctor's questions, I was still blotting pee from the front of my favorite peach pearl-cotton sweater using one of the extra cloth diapers I had packed in Sam's diaper bag. The doctor didn't seem to notice. I suppose he'd seen plenty of peed-on clothes. I would rather Sam had wet my blue jeans.

"You seem to be doing all right. Do you have any questions?" he asked.

"We're all right," I lied. "I don't have any questions. Wait. Yes I do. What do I do when I'm ready to go back to work or need to go out for a few hours?"

I felt panic rise inside my chest. Sam had one bottle in the hospital. The nurses filled it with water so I could get some sleep, but Sam spit it up. So the nurses felt obliged to wake me up anyway. Once, Mark warmed up a formula bottle to take a turn feeding Sam, but he threw that milk up, too. Would I ever get any rest?

"A lot of moms express their breast milk and store it so that baby can have it in a bottle when mom is out. I recommend you get in touch with La Leche League. They even rent moms a machine for that." He handed me a telephone number that he'd written on his notepad. "You're doing great, and we'll see you again when he's two months old and we start his immunizations," he said. I glanced at the note, trying to

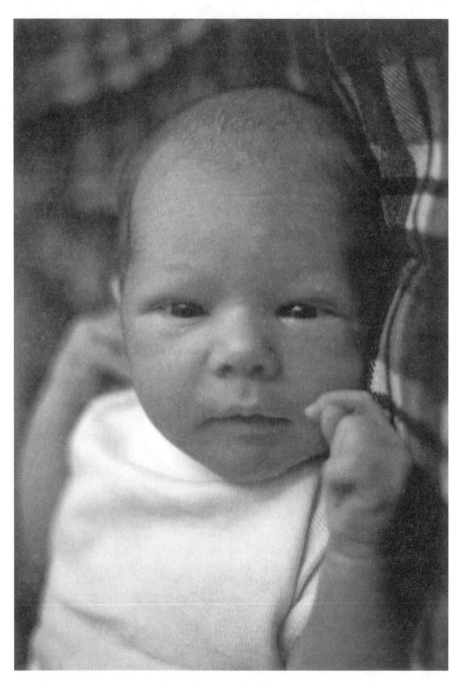

"I am restless."

remember if I'd read about those machines in any of my child-care books. By the time I looked up, he had left the examination room.

I snapped Sam's combed-cotton undershirt back on. This undershirt had become one of my favorite hand-me-downs, already soft and smelling familiar. The all-in-one shirt fastened together with three snaps at the bottom—a design that held the diaper ensemble together. We'd decided to use cloth diapers to save money. Instead of pins to secure the diapers, we bought nylon diaper covers with Velcro closures in fun colors. I adored Tuesday mornings. That was the day I put Sam's used diapers in a big baby-blue bag on the front stoop and the diaper service came and took them away, leaving behind a clean stash of diapers for the week ahead.

Sam fussed through all the poking, prodding, dressing, and undressing. I was getting better at it, but I was still clumsy. By the time I finished, Sam was wailing, which made me cry. Even before I had Sam, I cried easily. Happy endings or sad, I cried at movies. When I was seven and Chris was five, we'd both cried hysterically at the end of a National Geographic special on sea turtles as we watched seagulls fly in and eat the baby turtles before they could make it to the ocean. Even as a teenager, I cried watching the little boy happily get tackled by a dozen Labrador puppies in a commercial. Great music made me cry, too. Now that I had a baby, tears were always nearby.

I kept my eyes on the floor and hurried through the hospital clinic lobby as Sam and I both cried all the way out to the parking lot. Outside, I gave up trying to use the diaper bag to conceal the big wet spot on the front of my sweater. We both took a nap after we got home. Mine lasted an hour, and I felt much better. Sam's lasted nearly all day.

A few days later, I called the La Leche League. I told the woman who answered the phone that I wanted information about expressing milk so my husband could feed our baby when I was out. I was planning to take Sam to the gallery in Gold Discovery Park with me, but not every time. I told her my worries about whether Sam would ever accept a bottle. I impulsively asked a question I was afraid to ask anyone else.

"Do babies usually favor one breast over the other?" I blurted out.

"Some do," she replied. "It may be that the milk flows more easily from one side than from the other."

I began feeling brave enough to disclose more details of our freakish nursing relationship to a total stranger.

"Sam really favors the right side," I confessed. "I'm much bigger on the right than on the left."

"Usually we say to alternate which side you start on," she offered. "If you start one feeding on the right, then start the next feeding on the left. But you might want to start him on the left for each feeding for a while. You want him working that side when he's the hungriest so you're making more milk and so he gets used to working for it a bit more."

For about a month, I always started on the left side. But Sam adapted. He sucked hard until the milk let down and after the first few swallows, he'd let up and wait for me to switch him to the other side.

Eventually, I got the hang of expressing. I saw for myself that the left side had much less milk. It also seemed watery compared to the right.

I tried to tell the pediatrician about the nursing peculiarities at Sam's two-month checkup. But since Sam weighed in at twelve pounds, the outcome-oriented doctor was satisfied. He recommended soy instead of milk-based formula so that Sam wouldn't spit it up. Sam seemed to like the taste of soymilk. He finally accepted the occasional bottle from Mark, too. *Problem solved*, I thought.

For the next few months, before Sam was able to sit up on his own, I put him in a carryall, a hand-me-down from Chris. She said that she found it a great way to keep Ronnie nearby the first few months. She also recommended a windup swing to help Sam fall asleep, and a Johnny Jump Up to help tire him out when he was a few months older. Even though she was two years younger than me, she had three years more experience as a mother. I valued her suggestions. Yet she still seemed as bewildered as I was about Sam's long spells of fitful crying.

To keep his crying to a minimum, I took Sam almost everywhere in Chris's carryall, even to the bathroom when I took a shower. To keep him from fussing while I shampooed, I tied a windup plush toy to the carryall's handle so he had something to watch and hear. When he was about four months old, he accidentally kicked the toy. It jiggled. Sam smiled seeing his effect on the world. He kicked the toy over and over again. "You're a big boy, Sam." I laughed out loud.

Mark and I went on our first social outing with Sam early that spring. Mat and Jayne invited us to join them for Sunday brunch. They were friends of Mark's from the orchestra, and the only other couple in the group that had a baby. Doe-eyed, dark-haired Evan was several months older than Sam. Mat and Jayne had wanted us to meet them at a popular place in Sloughhouse, a little town southeast of Sacramento. I liked Sloughhouse. Its river-bottom farms filled with rows of sweet corn reminded me of Wisconsin. But I dreaded going out with Sam and told Mark so. We both knew that if he didn't sleep through brunch, he would cry until I nursed him. Mark reminded me that Mat and Jayne were open-minded and that nursing a baby was nothing to be ashamed or embarrassed about. I reminded Mark that when Sam was anxious, he hung on me like a leech.

Mat was the former personnel manager of the orchestra. When Mat left the personnel job, he had recommended Mark as his replacement, and that extra responsibility had doubled Mark's paycheck. Mark didn't want to decline Mat's invitation.

I offered little in the hour of conversation over *huevos rancheros*, giant buttermilk pancakes, hickory-smoked bacon, and crusty brown cubes of potatoes. Evan was old enough to sit in a high chair. Jayne played loving little baby games with Evan and helped him eat small bites of rice cereal from a vinyl-coated spoon.

Evan seemed content and happy, especially compared to Sam, who demanded my breast from the moment we sat down in the booth. Brunch was almost over before Mark noticed that I had eaten little from my own plate. He got up from the table and took Sam outside with him. Mat followed him, then Jayne and Evan a few minutes later.

Alone at the table, the red flush on my face cooled and the sweat under my breasts evaporated. I ate a few bites of cold blueberry pancakes and sage-scented sausage. It was probably satisfying food when it first came out of the kitchen, but now tasted like paste. Old food.

We walked the grounds of the restaurant after brunch. The deck overlooked a creek bed. The lowlands were greening with spring plantings. Trees shaded the deck and other warm, sunny spots were fine for lingering, but Sam began to cry. Mark passed him to me, hoping that would quiet him. I bounced Sam gently and tried talking to him in soothing tones. I'd dressed him for a cool day and snuck a glance at Evan, to see whether Jayne had bundled her baby up more than I had. I didn't realize that Mat had brought a video camera, and that he was filming us, until his narration drifted past my ears.

"Here's Peggy with Sam. He's nearly four months old. We just enjoyed a wonderful brunch here in Sloughhouse," Mat said.

Mark had kept up appearances for the three of us. I didn't like faking the picture-perfect image of motherhood, but I turned to the camera and did my best to give a warm smile.

Sure, let's save for posterity my writhing, wriggling baby, I thought. I knew from his cry that he was tired, too. I wanted to go home, put Sam in his crib to cry, and walk away. *He doesn't like being held anyway.*

I felt Mat and Jayne were politely ignoring Sam and me as we fumbled through breakfast. With Mat's camera pointed at us, we became the focus of attention. I'd had enough.

"The video is over now," I said flatly.

That ended the party. We said our good-byes. Mark whisked us into the car. I had embarrassed him, but I didn't care. Within a mile, Sam fell asleep and I was glad for the silence inside the car. I was angry at Mark for putting me through the pretense. Our world was far from perfect, and I couldn't pretend that it was. I knew in my heart that my anger meant more about me than it did about Mark, but I still fumed.

About a month later, Sam gave up on the left breast. I told myself that I didn't need to worry about it, because just like the doctor said, he's still growing. My left breast shrunk and my right breast swelled. I packed away my pretty peach sweater. I didn't wear anything else but "battle clothes," my moniker for sweats and other loose-fitting outfits suitable for spit-out food, spills, and other baby stains. I stopped wearing makeup, let my perm grow out, and cut my hair short.

As Sam grew over the next five months, he dwindled to one or two breast feedings per day. He didn't ask for it one day. I didn't even realize that we'd both forgotten until after he went to bed. I felt guilty. But I didn't want to wake him up. Mid-morning the next day, I brought Sam to my bedroom to lie down next to me. He latched on, took a swallow, made a face. He let go, rolled over and looked away.

I was bewildered. Was this how all babies stopped nursing? Or did my milk go sour? I sensed that Sam would never ask for my breast again. I was right. At ten months old, he stopped nursing. I bound myself and took hot showers for the next few days as my right breast shrunk to meet my left.

Sam was now too old to be swaddled, too big for the windup swing. Mark and I had no more ideas to calm him when he was upset. Some nights, we gave up, buckled him in his car seat and drove for miles, hoping he would fall asleep to the gentle drone of our tires pacing the well-groomed California freeways.

First Steps

As Sam grew from a baby to a toddler, he met enough developmental milestones that he stayed off the pediatrician's radar of concern. At six months, Sam sat up. At seven months, he crawled. At one year, he walked on his own. I marked these firsts by putting a sticker on his "Baby's First Year" calendar or making short entries in his baby book. Sam preferred walking to crawling, so from about eight months on, Sam would whine and gesture to Mark or me to lend him our fingers to better balance himself. We bent over and walked with Sam until our backs ached.

Sam's long and intense period of separation anxiety unnerved me. His godparents, Doug and Cheryl, were experienced

"Grandpa, you have no hair, just a head."

schoolteachers in Stockton and had two boys of their own. They often tried to allay our new-parent fears.

"That separation anxiety comes around seven or eight months, and it passes," Cheryl said. "Our boys cried like that, too."

"Brandon had the separation anxiety worse than Ryan," Doug said, and paused. "Or was it Ryan that had it worse?"

Cheryl tried to get Doug's memory straightened out, which got Doug telling another story. In minutes, our serious topic turned to laughter and we remembered why we asked Doug and Cheryl to be Sam's godparents.

Sam went through his worst patch of separation anxiety when he was eight months old, during our summer in central Michigan at Blue Lake Fine Arts Camp. It was a working summer vacation. Mark taught tuba campers all day. But since I taught euphonium and there were so few students, I worked only in the morning. We arranged for a teenaged daughter of another faculty member to watch Sam. At first, she was excited about the job, but the joy of playing with a cooing baby soon disintegrated. He screamed each morning when I left, and cried most of the time I was teaching. She had to push him in his stroller around the campgrounds for half the morning, since that was the only thing that kept him quiet. He made her summer miserable.

In Sacramento, babysitters who'd had one or two evenings with Sam politely turned me down when I called again. We tried a drop-in center, where the caregivers sent parents on their way with pagers. When we returned, they told us that Sam cried the whole time. They would have paged us, but they knew we were both performing in a concert. They were puzzled that Sam didn't tire himself out like other children. Seeing Sam's puffy, red eyes, I told Mark we'd never go back there.

One of the few places Sam seemed content was Jan and Tracy's house. They didn't have kids, but they did have Daphne, an energetic, affable cocker spaniel that trotted in and out her doggie door to the backyard all day long, performing what Sam thought was a great peekaboo game. When he wasn't watching Daphne's antics, Sam liked to crawl into Tracy's studio to play with the bass drum. Tracy would gently strike the drum with the foot pedal as Sam pressed his ear against the drum skin, listening to the sound vibrate and fade away. Jan and Tracy delighted in recounting Sam's adventures in their house. They thought Sam was really smart. Perhaps Sam's only problem was that he was precocious: nine months going on nineteen, Mark and I told each other.

For Sam's first birthday, we invited friends from birthing class to bring their one-year-olds over for a party. Between the living and dining rooms of our new home, an old California Craftsman house that we'd begun refurbishing, we had much more space for entertaining. Soon after everyone arrived, Sam put his head down on the living room floor and fell asleep. Although he didn't have a fever, his face was flushed. I picked him up, took him to his bedroom, and put him in his crib. Mark and I opened presents as Sam slept through the bedlam of a half-dozen noisy one-year-olds eating cake and drinking punch with all their parents and siblings.

Early Christmas morning that year, we drove to San Diego, checked into an upscale hotel, and enjoyed almost a whole wing to ourselves. We took Sam to the zoo the next day, thinking that a trip to the zoo would be more fun for him than presents under a Christmas tree. It was, until that evening. While looking for a coffee shop in La Jolla, Mark rear-ended an old Chrysler Imperial. The impact barely dented the Chrysler's bumper, but the jolt ruined the front end of our Subaru sedan and terrified Sam.

I thought a warm bath back at the hotel might calm him, but he kept whining and fouled the water. Mark helped clean the tub before collapsing in the easy chair. With the remote control, he flipped from channel to channel on the hotel television until I fell asleep. We moved to another, cheaper hotel the next day. Sam and I stayed there while Mark got the car fixed well enough for us to drive home. Friends asked us how our Christmas vacation turned out. I let Mark answer. His selective memory recounted a better Christmas than mine.

Since the families from birthing class had enjoyed our reunion at Sam's birthday party, another family arranged for a summer get-together at their new Roseville home. The house was so big and new they didn't even have furniture in half the rooms. All the other children played together on the patio except Sam. He wandered alone through the big house, pushing a chair up against the walls so that he could climb up and reach the light switches. He turned them on and off repeatedly. The hostess said she didn't mind. Mark told me to leave Sam be. But I kept running after him, carrying him back to the patio where the party was. He kicked and yelled. I was spoiling his fun.

For Sam's third Christmas, I couldn't bring myself to plan any celebration. If I bought Sam toys, he wouldn't play with them. He didn't play with the toys he had now. He wouldn't even play with the wrapping paper, bows, or empty boxes. He didn't notice when I began plugging in the big, multicolored tree lights, so I didn't bother finishing the decorations.

Christmas Day came and went. Mark spent the day as he wanted, practicing for another orchestra audition that he would take soon after the holidays. That night, as I crawled into bed next to Mark, I told myself not to think about the two Grinches who stole my Christmas. If I did, I would have cried myself to sleep.

Months were rolling into years, and those few times that Mark and I had talked about Sam's over-the-top temper tantrums and stilted language, Mark alternated between overcompensating for Sam and ignoring him. I chose not to write about the oddities in Sam's baby book, because then I didn't have to think about them, either.

But I knew better.

One night after Sam fell asleep, I joined Mark in cleaning the kitchen because I wanted to talk about Sam. For the past few months, I had become obsessed with figuring out why Sam couldn't talk. As Mark washed the dishes, I took them from him to dry and put away. I barraged Mark with theories, each needing a full exploration. Was it lead poisoning from all the dust kicked up renovating the house? Was it that glass of wine I drank and the sushi I ate before I'd known I was pregnant? Was Sam's brain damaged during those few minutes of labor when his heart rate slowed and I almost lost consciousness? Was there something in the air, something in the water? Still, I dared not bring up my darkest thought—that I had damaged myself in the clutches of that eating disorder, crashing my hormonal system and making my periods stop altogether.

Mark braced himself over the kitchen sink for a moment and then turned back to me. Tears filled up his clear blue eyes making them look tired and gray. "You know, sometimes," he stammered, "I just don't think ten fingers and ten toes is enough."

My heartbeat rattled my breastbone. It stopped any more words from reaching my mouth.

We finished the dishes in silence.

First Friends

Sam slept until eight or nine in the morning, which gave me one or two precious hours to clean the house or get some arts council work done before caring for him consumed the rest of my day. I had to help him dress and make his breakfast. He could undress himself better than he could dress himself. He could feed himself, but he ignored his spoon and fork. Still, he ate a healthy breakfast—whole-grain pancakes or waffles, fresh berries, scrambled eggs, and smoothies.

For juice and smoothies, I bought a bottle-to-cup system I had seen in Japan. My mentor's daughter, Akiko, was a toddler. I had enjoyed watching Akiko grow and change. Even though Akiko wasn't quite two years old, Toru and Chieko had encouraged her to pick up grains of rice with chopsticks. Akiko also liked to play with me. Occasionally, I understood her Japanese better than that of the adults, but she couldn't pronounce my name. As I tried to learn Japanese myself, I figured out that my name didn't fit in the natural building blocks of the Japanese alphabet. Akiko adapted by taking the sound of the first letter, *P*, and adding the honorary suffix, *san*, to be polite. My name was *Pe-san* when we played. Akiko's favorite cup had been a short, sturdy one with white handles on both sides. Chieko showed me the different options for its top— with a quick twist, the cup changed from a bottle-style nipple to a sipper, to a straw, to a covered top with a small hole to slow down spills.

Sam liked his cup with the straw-top best. He enjoyed breakfast smoothies from juice squeezed out of the oranges off the tree in our backyard, which I whirred in the blender with bananas and yogurt. Sometimes, I snuck in pinches of wheat germ and brewer's yeast for an extra dose of vitamin B.

"I am going to go out the dog door. I did that when I was little."

After finishing his breakfast, Sam would run to the front door. With or without me, rain or shine, Sam would fly out the door for his morning walk.

He would leap down the three stairs of our concrete stoop to the driveway, with me trying to catch up, still pulling up the heel on the back of my sandal.

"Wait for me, Sam!" I would yell, to no avail. I would run several steps to catch up as he lunged down the driveway and turned onto the sidewalk. Every morning we scrambled down Sherman Way, past the many 1930s-era Craftsman houses that made up our neighborhood. At San Jose Way, Sam would turn right past the mini-Tudor home of the orchestra's principal bassist and his wife. Most of the mornings we breezed by, they were still sleeping.

Sam turned right again on Y Street. The lots on Y Street had been laid out more generously, making it more than a quarter mile to circle our block. The houses were older and bigger, too. They were built before the first wave of urban sprawl brought more, and smaller, houses to our neighborhood. One retired man kept his wide-blade grass cut meticulously, pushing his rotary-blade lawn mower under a small grove of mature palm trees at least once a week. Whenever I saw him tending his lawn, I smiled at him and we waved to each other.

Sam never noticed the man or his mower. He just went on.

Once we went past the neighbor woman with whom we shared our back fence. She was stripping honey from several beehives with the help of a few friends.

"Don't worry. They're really docile right now," she called out as we walked by. Her smoking pots were all around the hives. Everyone in the group was wearing long sleeves and pants, but no other special protection. Instantly, I knew why, in late fall, Sam stepped on so many dead and dying bees in our backyard.

"Okay, thanks," I called back.

Sam didn't notice the smoke or the bees. He just went on.

At the end of Y Street, we'd walk past a dusty Chevy Chevette parked on the other side. The tires on the little blue car were flat and it never moved from its spot. One day, as we walked by the car, a twentysomething man came out of the house and down the porch carrying a baseball bat. With a big swing, he smashed the front windshield. He looked up and seemed surprised to see me and Sam.

"It's okay," he called. "It doesn't run anymore." My own startled look softened and I smiled. *Sometimes, I'd like to put a baseball bat through a car window*, I thought. *My career's going nowhere; I'm thirty and pregnant—accidentally, again; and I can't keep up with the toddler I have.*

Sam turned right for a short sprint on Miller Street and right again for the final stretch down Sherman Way. Cutting across our tiny front lawn of Bermuda grass lined with Shasta daisies that were always flopped over, Sam rounded the fragrant, white star jasmine vine I'd planted. He jumped up the stairs to the front door and let himself in. The welcome end of another chase-Sam-around-the-block episode for me. But for Sam, it was his morning espresso.

Sam's morning dash gave him the chance to look at things—fences, bushes, stone walls—out of the corner of his eye as he flew by them. He wasn't looking for anyone to be his friend.

First Words

Something about the way Sam related to me didn't feel right, either. At the kitchen counter, he took my hand and raised it toward the cookie jar for a cookie. At the sink in the corner, he

"Mom's swimming while holding me."

raised my hand for a drink of water. At the front door, he raised my hand to ask for a walk around the block.

"Well, Patti said to make him use the word, make him tell you before you give him things," Mark said one night after a phone conversation with his stepmother about Sam.

She's in Houston, I thought, *and she hasn't seen him for months now. How could she know that he's not being willful?*

We'd become so confused that we had considered wilder advice than Patti's. I tried the suggestion anyway.

"Do you want a cookie, Sam?" I asked after he took me to the cookie jar.

He grabbed my hand and pushed it toward the jar again. I pulled out a snickerdoodle, his favorite, and held it before him.

"Say 'cookie' Sam," I insisted.

No words magically came out. But the look of betrayal welling up in his chocolate brown eyes was wrenching. *Sam needs to trust me*, I thought, and I abruptly handed over the cookie crackled with cinnamon and sugar.

A few weeks later, I picked up a free parenting magazine from the rack at Java Joe's and took it home so I could read a short article about language development. If your child didn't have language by the age of two, the deficit could affect the future development of his brain, the article quoted the expert. Call your county office of education, the article advised.

The first wave I'd been swimming against for two years hit: Sam was not going to grow out of whatever it was that descended upon him. It was going to get worse.

I opened to the blue-lined pages of the telephone book and found the number for the Sacramento county office of education.

"How old is your son?" the unidentified person on the other end asked.

"He's about two and a half," I answered. *Breathe in, breathe out*, I coached myself.

"We have about a six-month waiting list for services, Mrs. Wolfe," Anonymous said. "By the time we get to him, he may already be three years old and in the jurisdiction of the school district."

"I don't understand. I read somewhere that you could help," I said as distinctly as I could. "Please, he's already two and a half and he doesn't talk."

"Well, I suppose we can still schedule an intake appointment and get things started," Anonymous said. "I'll have someone call you."

We both hung up. *Victory*, I thought.

A few days later, the phone rang and a quiet, probing voice identified herself as Nancy, a speech therapist from the county office of education.

"In order for us to best help your son, we start by doing a short evaluation," she explained. "We bring some toys and books to your home and watch him play for a while. Would that be all right?"

"Sure," I answered. What does playing with toys reveal to a speech therapist? If they handed him a car, he wouldn't push it around, saying "vroom, vroom." Sam would turn it upside down, spin the wheels, and stare into the vibrating illusion of mass.

"I can come next week Thursday afternoon. Another evaluator will come with me. It should take about an hour, maybe a little more. Will one o'clock be okay?" she asked.

"Sure," I answered.

The whirlwind scheduled for Thursday at one o'clock began with oodles of toys, books, and pictures Sam hadn't seen before. The two women worked gently, yet quickly, trading tasks and challenges to keep Sam moving. Of course, he examined the toys for things that could spin, or parts that opened and closed. Does this make noise? I could see him asking himself. He didn't have much use for the picture vocabulary cards. He flapped one up and down, watching it out of the corner of his eye.

"It will take us about two weeks to work up the results," Nancy said after they finished. "And can you fill out this parent report? It will be part of the evaluation. I will call you to schedule another visit when we're ready."

I took the packet that she held out to me. There were many questions. I could see that some would take time to research. At Sam's baby shower, my girlfriends had given me that calendar to mark his milestones with a sticker. Sit up, crawl, first words, first steps—all had been marked on the date with a sticker. I'd grown to hate making entries in his baby book. The energy I had before Sam was born, when I wrote paragraphs anticipating his arrival, was gone now. Writing down Sam's achievements felt fraudulent. "First time waved good-bye," the report asked with a short blank line by the phrase. How would I have described that day when he was eight months old? Sitting high in Mark's arms, eager for a walk to the grocery store at the corner of Colonial and Stockton, Sam had waved at me from the doorway. Clearly overwhelmed by our joyous reaction to his new skill, he stopped. And he refused to wave again for months. Did that count? Was that the first official time he began waving bye-bye? Does he have to keep waving bye-bye in order to get credit for it on the county office of education's parent report?

"Okay," I said to Nancy. She gave me instructions where to mail the report when I was finished.

Nancy came by herself several weeks later carrying her dark vinyl satchel. She pulled out a manila file with "Wolfe,

Samuel D." written in the color-coded tab on the top. Inside were several copies of a two-page report. She gave me one stamped "Copy." The little report touched on many things: receptive and expressive language, self-help, social skills, educational aptitude, and achievement. Every category of evaluation had several sentences that summed up an hour of playing with Sam. The report gave us new words and phrases and ideas for describing Sam, such as *skill scatter*. He was markedly ahead of his age on some tasks, but terribly behind on others. Socially, the report said, he was at the level of a six-month-old baby.

"His language deficits qualify him for speech services," Nancy said. "That's about all the county can offer you right now. I can come for a visit once per week and work with you and Sam on developing his language. He can probably get more from the school district when he turns three."

"That's great," I said. "But I'm not sure what to think about all this other information and what to do about it."

"Sometimes when you work in one domain, it helps the others," she said.

"Oh." I was skeptical that learning to say the word *potty* would help Sam develop a desire to use it, but I took her observation as hopefully as it was offered.

"Could you keep track of all the words he uses this week and write them down?" Nancy asked. "It might be a good place to start."

"Sure, I think I could do that. There really aren't that many," I said.

Nancy slipped the manila folder with Sam's name on it back into her satchel. As she stood up and we started toward the front door, I turned to Sam. He was putting the rainbow-colored doughnuts back on the stacking spindle.

"Nancy's leaving, Sam. Would you like to tell her bye-bye?" I asked.

Nancy and I looked at Sam as he abandoned the stacking toy on the living room floor and disappeared into his bedroom. I shrugged my shoulders and offered Nancy a slight smile. Nancy smiled back. She seemed to have as much hope as I did. But I wondered how she could get him to talk.

"See you next week," she said.

"Next week," I echoed, and watched her through the picture window as she put her satchel in the trunk of her sedan. As she stepped into the driver's seat, another car raced by before she pulled away herself. She drove down Sherman Way where it ended at Stockton Boulevard in front of the medical center, where either left or right would be her next house call to another mom who was wondering how she failed to help her child learn to talk.

Well, I thought, *Sam knows* "bye-bye." I went back to the corner of the kitchen where we'd set up the home office. I got a piece of white paper from the computer printer and a pen from the desk drawer. "Sam's Words" I wrote at the top and dated it.

"Bye-bye, go," I wrote down the side of the paper.

Theodor Geisel's publisher made a bet with him. Could he write a beginner book using just fifty words? Geisel took the challenge, of course.

"Cookie, Sam, Dad, Mom," I wrote.

Copies of the little book's manuscript hung on the museum wall. Clearly, Geisel was counting his words as he worked out his poetry. "I would not like them here or there. I would not like them anywhere."

"Water, drink, walk," I wrote.

"I do not like green eggs and ham."

"Bee, ouch," I wrote. I listened to Sam all week. Once in a while, I logged a new word. The day before Nancy was scheduled to visit, I double-checked my count.

"I do not like them, Sam-I-am."

Fifty. He had fifty words in all.

"I am Sam. Sam I am."

Favorite Toys

"HE'S GOT SOME VERBS HERE. That's something," Nancy said, adjusting her glasses to look through the list of fifty words. She explained that Sam was almost a year behind in normal language development. "It won't be as hard since he's using some verbs. We want to work toward some combinations, like 'Car go.' You know, simple two-word sentences."

She handed the list back to me.

"Does Sam imitate you?"

"What do you mean?"

"When you talk, does he ever repeat what you say?"

"No. I guess I never realized it before, but no," I replied. "My god, Nancy, how can I teach him to imitate me?"

"Let's not worry about that right now. I brought a video for you and Mark to watch. It has some basic techniques to elicit speech."

From her satchel, she pulled out a tape inside a simple white box.

"I want to show you one idea from the tape," she said.

Nancy had put a bead roller coaster on the floor before she looked over Sam's fifty-word list. Sam was already moving a

"It's my first day to walk."

line of yellow beads up and down the thick, cherry-red wire mounted on a sturdy pine base. She sat next to him and began to narrate his play in the same quiet, deliberate way she had first talked with me on the phone. I had seen that kind of toy only a few times before. Even as an adult, I found moving the beads felt soothing and purposeful.

"Look, Sam, you're making those yellow beads go up and down. You're making them go up. Now you're letting them fall down. That's fun, Sam," Nancy said.

She turned to me.

"Just describe what he's doing. He'll make the connections between the words you're using and what they're for. This toy is good for eye-hand coordination and visual tracking—the kind of motor skills he will need to learn to read."

I began to wonder whether I was Sam's problem. Of course, Sam wasn't talking because I wasn't a chatty mother. My quiet love wasn't enough. *I should be walking up and down the aisles of the grocery store going on about red apples, and green peas, and orange oranges*, I thought. *That must be why he doesn't know his colors*. I didn't coo. I didn't baby talk. I didn't refer to myself in the third person.

But I still couldn't understand. The world around us was noisy enough.

Over the next few months, Nancy helped unleash more words from Sam. I made myself talk about everything we encountered, even about inane things. Sam's speech became chunkier. He repeated large phrases, whole sentences. For Sam, language was like a thousand-piece puzzle that someone had already put together and returned to the puzzle box with big, fat sections still intact. He might recognize a section and put it in the right place. I had to fill in the gaps of individual pieces of speech that were missing.

Now that I knew how to play with Sam, I spent more time with him just playing on the floor. I saw Mark shared my enthusiasm. Sam understood more of what Mark and I said to him than first we thought, at least in a general way. When I asked Sam if he wanted to go to the store, he knew where we were going.

While Sam's communication skills improved, his behavior did not. If we waited in a restaurant foyer for carryout, Sam had a meltdown. He couldn't stand being in a checkout line. If something bothered him in public, he'd erupt. Mark and I often quizzed each other during meals or while running errands, trying to figure out what set Sam off. Since he didn't throw a tantrum for the same reasons as other toddlers, such as being denied a toy or treat, we often argued about what caused his meltdowns or what was the best way to stop them.

Even when Sam was content, he elicited rude looks and heartless comments from strangers. He wiggled and whined like a normal kid, but with a sharper edge. At the corner grocery one day, a man waiting in line at the cash register became angry with Sam's wiggling and whining. "If you don't shut that kid up and keep him still, I'll kill him," he said with an eerie calm. Stunned by the threat, I could only stare at the man. I pulled Sam in and held him close. The horrified clerk moved the angry man through the checkout line as fast as he could.

Yet, Sam behaved well enough at Fowler's Toys—a place where we always felt welcome. A newspaper story said that the owner planned her toy store for a long time before opening on 24th and J streets. Mrs. Fowler had a mission for her inventory. If the toy had been advertised on television, you wouldn't find it in her store, the story said.

Sam and I often went shopping on the foggiest gray days of the rainy season, opening her glass door into a clean, brightly colored toy land. Mrs. Fowler set up play areas inside her cozy store, allowing me the freedom to explore while Sam played. I studied what she had on her shelves, thinking about what I was learning from Nancy, and picked out toys for Sam that might help him catch up.

I bought a lot.

I bought thick, pliable puzzles that came apart in four or five pieces and took endless wear and tear. "Dog!" "Elephant!" "Truck!" Sam would say as he popped in the last piece.

I bought a wooden train with rickety tracks and an extension that made a little hill. "Train goes up and down, up and down." Sam echoed my narration as he pushed the track halfway under his bed. He giggled when he pulled the train back around the track and out of the bed's shadow.

I bought several bug puppets, and another puppet that turned from a tadpole to a frog and back again. "Fly, fly," Sam urged a ladybug puppet, as he moved it up and down in the air.

Sam and I were shopping one day when a shipment arrived. Mrs. Fowler called out to a co-worker, "I've been waiting for these for a while. Aren't these fun?"

She held up a push toy that looked like a rotary-blade lawn mower with a round, wooden cage linked with two red wheels. Inside the cage, four big beads, painted in primary colors, and one giant jingle bell bounced. The handle was the right height for Sam.

I bought that, too.

Sam pushed the noisy mower around the oak floors of our house and atop the concrete driveway in our backyard until the paint chipped away and the wheels fell off.

"Round and round," he repeated to himself.

Fowler's carried beautiful children's books. Sam wore out several pop-up books I bought for him. *Nature's Hidden World* was a favorite. He lifted the flap to see the worm and pushed the tab to make the frog eggs hatch. I would read the book and try to narrate Sam's flap-lifting and tab-pushing at the same time. Sam didn't seem to understand the words in the books, so I could only wonder what he connected to.

During her many trips abroad, Mark's mother found miniature-print editions of several Eric Carle books. She mailed them to Sam. He enjoyed touching the illustrations, especially the raised web made by *The Very Busy Spider* and the holes chewed by *The Very Hungry Caterpillar*. He also responded to the gentle repetition in Carle's texts, which were similar to stories by Margaret Wise Brown that I had remembered from my own childhood. But it wasn't until I brought home *Dr. Seuss's ABC* that a story came alive for Sam. He loved the rhythm of Geisel's poetry and would listen—really listen—as we turned the pages.

I hoped Nancy could help us figure out why Sam screamed so much. I told her that there didn't seem to be a relationship between his frustration and the volume of his voice. When he yelled after a block fell from the stack he built, it was just as loud as when I put him in his high chair for lunch. I wondered whether he was frustrated, always adapting his Spartan world of language to ours, and that frustration fueled his raging vocal cords. But for all I knew, he liked the sound of his voice bouncing between the living room walls.

Sam's screams pounded on my eardrums and fed my frustration with his behavior. If there was a way to make him stop, I couldn't find it. I read positive parenting books trying to find the solution. Once, in desperation, I tried spanking him. He turned around and looked baffled. *He thinks I hit him for no reason*, I thought. I realized Sam made no connection between his yelling and my spanking. It didn't matter that the television was off, that Mark practiced tuba out in the studio, and that ours was a quiet house. Sam's volume was insanity. I had no peace when he was awake.

"*I do not like this one so well. All he does is yell, yell, yell,*" I once recited to myself in the loudest voice I could. Dr. Seuss's illustration said it all—bright yellow eyes closed, red nose, mouth wide open with bold, black sound waves reverberating to the margins of the page.

Sam lifted his head. I turned to meet his sideways gaze. I held my breath. His eyes filled with tears. *Oh my god*, I thought. *His language has come so far. How could I be so careless?* In the window of his eyes, I saw he got the worst meaning of the passage. How could I tell my funny little boy that I love him with all my heart, just as he is, yells and all?

"*This one is quiet as a mouse. I like to have him in the house,*" I offered, but it was too late.

"I'm sorry, Sam. I didn't mean it," I said softly. "I love you, sweetie."

Sam's wide, wizened eyes told me his oddball ways didn't mean he couldn't be hurt. I had no idea how to make reparations. Even though Sam forgave me, I was having a hard time forgiving myself. Nancy's help gave Sam a few more lines, but I kept messing up my parenting part.

I was beginning to feel alone on stage.

Before Sam was born, I used to jog with Mark, sometimes in the morning, sometimes late at night after he came home from rehearsal. We showered off the sweat, made love, and got all sweaty again. Now that we had another baby on the way, I couldn't jog with Mark anymore.

When I was pregnant, I felt like my body separated into parts and my belly was too heavy to keep up. However, I knew if I didn't do something to feel fit instead of fat, I couldn't keep my head in check. I bought a membership at the midtown Y where I could exercise and unwind. The other health clubs in town had a meat market scene, but not the Y. We Rubenesque women all followed a quiet routine in changing clothes, showering, and lowering ourselves into the cool, clean, buoyant waters of that ancient pool—meditation in freestyle, meditation in backstroke.

Once I got home, though, the calm flipped to Sam's chaos. Mark couldn't, or wouldn't, handle time alone with Sam. I began to lose my perspective, almost believing that one hour's respite was the same as child neglect and abandonment.

Gail, a friend from birthing class who also volunteered to watch Sam occasionally, suggested a girls' day out in Calistoga one mid-summer morning. We invited Jan and another young mom, who was a friend of Jan's. The four of us spent more time driving through the wine country to get to Calistoga than we did relaxing in the mud baths. I returned to Sacramento before dark with home-spa supplies and a fresh attitude.

It didn't last. Mark was so upset for leaving him alone with Sam all day that he refused to talk to me that evening. He wouldn't say why.

I let the silence simmer, even though I boiled with anger. Everyone else we knew with toddlers had a life, plus babysitting options. On the rare weekend I got to go out, I was usually sitting alone in the concert hall, listening to Mark and the Sacramento Symphony play a concert that was important to him. *How dare he? Sam is his son, too. I work hard to make a living, too.* We had agreed before Sam was born that we were both going to become successful parents, but it didn't happen. Sam's care had become my exclusive responsibility.

Sam and I had our daily routine. Mark had his. He got up each morning and ran several miles. He'd shower, make himself a huge plate of Mexican eggs—fried eggs and refried beans with jack cheese and imported Mexican salsa he bought in a can. Over breakfast, he would read the sports pages. He'd head to the studio we converted from the garage and practice for several hours. If he needed to do a little personnel work in the office, he'd leave in the early afternoon, and come back for supper before heading to the night's rehearsal or concert.

"Mark, please help me more with Sam," I begged, again, one morning. "I can't get anything else done if you're unavailable until one o'clock in the afternoon."

"Just put him in the studio with me," he said. "You know I've got to practice, and I don't mind if he's in there. Plus, he has a good time."

While Sam enjoyed being in the studio, I didn't want to give Mark credit for the idea. Mark practiced excerpts for auditions a lot, which meant he played the same small lines of music over and over. It was monotonous. Somehow, the offer seemed small compared to my frustration with the two of them. But I accepted it, and I didn't give anyone the chance to look over my shoulder and tell me that I'd made another decision that wasn't good enough for my child. Instead, I chose to think of it as our miniature version of Take Your Child to Work Day.

Many mornings, I opened the studio door and left Sam inside the room to run around as Mark practiced. I knew Sam wouldn't interrupt Mark and Mark wouldn't play with him either.

On a late-night trip to San Francisco to pick Mark up at the airport after an audition for another orchestra, Sam had yet another tantrum. I didn't know the cause, but we had half the trip still ahead of us. I started singing an athletic line from Respighi's *Fountains of Rome* that Mark practiced a lot. Sam smiled, squealed, and kicked his legs in rhythm on the edge of the car seat. To keep him happy, I sang tuba parts for at least thirty miles.

Sam's bedtime routine took its toll, too. I had to lie down with him each night, often a half hour or more, until he relaxed enough to fall asleep. His hair had grown in a soft, smooth, and sun-kissed blonde, but he wouldn't let me cuddle him or stroke his hair to help him relax. Some nights his routine stretched to hours. Mark complained bitterly, since we used to spend his evenings off playing duets together. As musicians we were insatiable, pushing the boundaries of our instruments and exploring all kinds of music. But most nights now, by the time I emerged from Sam's bedroom, Mark and I were too tired to play.

Sam and I had memorized the gentle rhythms of *Goodnight Moon*. We recited the little poem every night to help him relax. Before we finished wishing goodnight to the stars, and the air, and noises everywhere, we often interrupted that last big chunk of speech. Sam inserted a goodnight to the mailman, or the dog, or the honeybees, or whatever was part of the drama of his day. Most nights he added, "Goodnight, Mom. Goodnight, Dad."

One night, I got up from the bed thinking that Sam was fast asleep. He awoke, frightened and fitful that I was leaving him alone in the room. I lay back down. Each time he drifted off and I rose from the bed, he woke up again. No amount of cooing or coaxing helped him to sleep. Finally, exhausted, I stood up. Sam was crying. So was I.

"*Today is gone. Today was fun*," I said with tears rolling down my cheeks. His face relaxed. His eyes looked straight into mine. Although I was almost overwhelmed by the unfamiliar feeling of his full gaze, I continued, wiping my cheeks with my shirt. "*Tomorrow is another one.*"

He smiled as I straightened out his comforter around him and let my voice decrescendo. "*Every day, from here to there, . . .*"

"*. . . funny things are everywhere*," he finished.

Preschool Memories

Sam's third birthday loomed, which meant we had to say good-bye to Nancy and her home visits. The county ran the infant development programs, but once children turned three years old, Sacramento City Unified School District assumed responsibility.

Their special education staff insisted that Sam be evaluated again, even though the county had evaluated him only six months earlier. They wouldn't test Sam in the comfort of our living room, either. Instead, we were sequestered in a small room at an old elementary school near Goethe Park. I was grateful for winter sunshine coming through the short, wide window at the far end of the room. Was this once someone's office, and had they enjoyed looking up from their desk at the leaves on the trees outside? In Sacramento, leaves clung to trees through fall and winter. In Wisconsin, maple, oak, and elm trees turned blazing red and orange before the leaves piled high on the ground and left tree skeletons behind.

For part of the testing, the speech therapist and the educational diagnostician paired up to save time. Instead of the graceful

"I used to play with toys in the sandbox."

exchange Nancy and her colleague had during Sam's first evaluation, these two educators often asked Sam to do the same thing at separate times, such as "Give me the red block" or "Write your name." When Sam failed to do what he was asked, the temperature of the tiny room rose.

No matter what they asked, Sam tried to respond in his own way, which could be attributed to our hard work so far. Before, Sam often would have simply ignored them. Watching them plod through their list of tasks was trying my patience. Their tests twisted, turned, and stopped at dead ends.

By the time the psychologist arrived to do his own independent evaluation, Sam had retreated to the corner of the room, flipping the light switch—off, on, off, on, off, on, off, on. What was Sam trying to figure out about the switch and that dim light bulb in the ceiling? The psychologist didn't seem interested in Sam's behavior. Instead, he spoke to Mark and me, asking the same old questions about Sam's birth or when he first waved bye-bye. Occasionally, the psychologist called Sam from the light switch to perform some task, such as "point to your nose" or "look at a picture" of something unfamiliar, asking him, "What is this, Sam?"

We escaped the small room late in the afternoon.

"It sure didn't seem like they knew what they were doing," I said.

"They weren't very organized," Mark agreed. "But they discovered stuff Sam couldn't do."

"Yeah? Well, we knew that he couldn't do things!" I snapped. "That's why we were there in the first place."

I began to vent.

"Why couldn't one person observe and note what the other was doing? Or just take our word for it? That was hard on Sam to be asked to do something again, by a different person, after he clearly couldn't do it the first time."

"I guess," Mark said.

"Like when the speech therapist put that gorgeous white teacup right in front of Sam—I mean right in front of him, as if she were handing it to him. And then she said, 'Now, Sam, don't touch this.' What the hell was that?"

"I don't know, babe. I don't know. But it's done now. Let's just go home and let Sam play outside in the backyard while we get some dinner on the grill," he said.

The trout we bought at the Sunday farmer's market under the freeway had marinated in soy sauce brine all day. I didn't know whether we'd have much time to cook, so I planned to toss it in the backyard smoker with a few applewood chips and garnish it with capers. That way, we could still enjoy a nice meal.

I watched Mark strap Sam into his car seat and close the door.

"You honestly think they'll have some insight?"

He picked up on my skepticism.

"Just drop it," he said.

On the way home, I turned the day's events over and over in my head like a Rubik's Cube. I couldn't let go the way Mark did. I wanted to know when anyone planned on getting to the point where we helped Sam catch up.

A few weeks later, Mark and I returned to the school. We sat around a big table with more people than had evaluated Sam. Each evaluator—the nurse, the psychologist, the speech therapist, the educational diagnostician—delivered a report on Sam's test scores. The results showed him hopelessly behind other children his age in many areas. The extra people looked on with interest and nodded. The evaluators made a number of links, saying Sam was "bright," but he couldn't "take directions." He was "easily irritated," but "enjoyed turning the light switch off and on." The supervisors continued to nod, but no one was coming to any kind of conclusion Mark or I could understand. Was anyone going to say Sam was mentally retarded or would they pick some softer term?

The speech therapist took her turn. "And Sam could not identify the parts of his body."

Why are these people telling me things I already know? I couldn't listen anymore.

"But what does that mean? I saw it. I saw it when you asked him to point to his nose and he didn't. Why is it important that he point to it when you ask him?"

I waited for an answer, some new nugget of information that would make that long day worthwhile.

"I don't know, Mrs. Wolfe," someone replied.

The speech therapist looked embarrassed. Mark looked mortified. All the polished presenters seated around the table fell silent.

Just like Dad, I could stop a conversation with a question. I'd been in this spot many times before. Somehow I corner people with my questions. Many specious fights between Mark and me started with one of my questions. No one held a gavel around this table, but they obviously understood the rules of the meeting. I didn't. *Someone needs to hand parents a copy of* California's Rules of Special Education Order *before the big day, I thought.*

"I'm sorry, Mrs. Wolfe," she said. "I'll try to find out for you."

I kept quiet while they finished presenting their plan for educating Sam. They proposed a daily special education preschool class at a nearby elementary school. They said the special education teacher also took her students once a week to the "parent-participation preschool," held in the portable building next to the school so they could interact with other children.

The stumped speech therapist phoned me about ten days later.

"Hello, Mrs. Wolfe."

"Um, hello," I replied. So many teachers, therapists, and evaluators had come in and out of our lives in the last six months that I couldn't connect her name to the database of Sam's handlers that I tried to store in my head.

"I called one of my professors from college to find out more about your question."

"What question was that?" I was rolling through my database.

"Your question about why he couldn't point to his nose," she answered.

"Oh, yes, yes, that." *A match*, I thought. "What did your professor say?"

"He said that Sam would have picked those words up from context. If you'd say, for example, 'Here's a tissue, Sam. Let's blow your nose,' eventually enough of those kinds of references go by and he recognizes that *nose* is the word for his nose," she said, her voice brimming with triumph.

"I see. That's quite helpful information," I said. "Thank you for going to the trouble to find out and call me."

"Well, it bothered me that I didn't know the answer to your question. I should have, but I didn't."

"Thanks. I appreciate your conscientiousness."

We hung up. I looked around the kitchen. *I've got to put labels on everything in this house*, I thought. I picked up a stack of self-adhesive labels from our computer printing supplies.

I started with a label on the light switch.

Playmates

Sam's preschool room was pleasant enough. One wall was lined with windows. The teacher, Mrs. Vargas, had a computer in the corner with a few games that taught the alphabet, math concepts, and counting. She seldom let Sam or the other eight children, all boys, use the computer. I could tell that Nick had Down's syndrome and Max had cerebral palsy. I couldn't tell what the other children's disabilities were. I didn't ask because I'd recently learned another one of the California Rules of Special Education Order: We Don't Label A Child. They put the policy in place, ostensibly, because labels impose artificial limits upon children.

Mrs. Vargas was excited about the new, whole-language method of readying children for reading. She read books like *Brown Bear, Brown Bear, What Do You See?* to the boys each day as they sat on carpet squares in a circle around her. She bought editions with pages as big as movie posters, and pointed to the giant-print words as she read them. Some of the books dwarfed Russell and John, the smallest boys in the class. *Maybe they were preemies*, I thought.

Mrs. Vargas complained that Sam wouldn't sit on a carpet square with his classmates during circle time. I went to school one day and watched Sam walk around the circle, sometimes stealing a glance at the book Mrs. Vargas was reading. I told her after circle time that I observed Sam trying to listen even though he couldn't sit still.

"Maybe you shouldn't worry that he can't sit still yet during circle time," I said.

"But he'll need to sit at a desk in kindergarten," she countered.

Conformist, I thought, shocking myself.

"I am happy to be outside. I like the outdoors."

One of Sam's classmates needed a diaper change. Neither Mrs. Vargas nor the aide seemed to notice the stink. I sneaked a glance at Sam's diaper. Clean and dry. No one changed whoever was dirty that day. I told Mark about it. Neither of us wanted Sam to ever spend his morning with dirty pants. We agreed to tag-team as volunteers, making a point not to miss the days that Sam and the other boys attended the parent-participation preschool.

The days that Sam and the other boys mixed in with the "normal" preschoolers at the portable were stressful for him. Teachers had organized the parent-participation preschool into stations. There was a building-blocks area, a bead-play area, and a toddler-sized kitchen, and, on special occasions, a water-play station. Parents supervised each play station.

My habit of narrating play, learned from Nancy, attracted kids to areas where I was stationed because they liked to have their play narrated, too. All the children, the "normal" and the "unlabeled," beamed as I described the action in their play. For once, I felt good as a parent. If I was stationed in the sandbox or the water-play area, where Sam liked to hang out, I'd watch him dig in the sand or scoop up water. But if he wandered into any other play area where I was stationed, he didn't stay long. Children bouncing from place to place, chattering and yelling— that was too much for Sam. And me, too. My ears rang all afternoon. The play-station ideas were inspired by Maria Montessori's theories. Yet I couldn't imagine that parents and teachers at those private schools with long waiting lists allowed such rowdiness.

Sam seemed better able to absorb new concepts in the small groups organized by the speech therapist. She stopped by the room every day to take one child, sometimes two, to her room to blow bubbles and confront vocabulary cards. I watched once.

Sam blew bubbles, but had trouble with the cards. She showed him a card with a picture of a hamburger on it that day.

"What's this, Sam?" she asked.

He walked around the speech therapist, looked at the card, and said nothing.

"What's this, Sam?" she repeated.

He started wandering away.

"Can you tell me what this is, Sam?" she repeated.

"I'm sorry," I whispered to her, pointing at the picture. "But he's never seen one of those before, let alone eaten one. I don't think he even knows the word *hamburger*."

"Oh, well," she said, putting the card down. "We try to get him to learn new words, too, not just say the words he knows."

Eventually, I learned all of the Rules by violating them one by one.

Height and Weight

"Hi, Mom. It's me," I telephoned.

"Hi, you," she replied. Sometimes hearing her voice was like stepping into a steaming, hot bath. My tension and worries evaporated. I was so glad that Mom and Dad returned early from Saudi Arabia. After Iraq invaded Kuwait in late 1990, Western newspapers claimed World War III was on the horizon. Chris and I, and our other sisters, Karen and Teresa, begged my parents to come home. Mom and Dad didn't understand our concerns. I was surprised Karen couldn't convince them that Saudi state-owned media was downplaying the invasion. But, within days of our panicked, trans-Atlantic phone calls, hundreds of F-16s flew in all night long over the compound where Mom and Dad lived. The next morning, Mom

"I liked watering the garden. I still do. I filled the holes with water."

packed her suitcases and came home. Dad fulfilled his contract with the clinic to earn his five-figure bonus. He returned home a few weeks later, before Iraqi missiles started landing in Riyadh and before our next baby was due, at the end of February.

"Mom, didn't you have Montessori stuff around when we were kids?" I asked.

"Oh, yes, but not a lot. I went to this short workshop and we discussed some of her writings, and we made things for our kids," she said.

Mom always questioned mainstream thinking. She had breastfed me and my three sisters at a time when doctors recommended formula feeding. In New London, she had served us hippie food like honey, whole-wheat bread, brown rice, and savory meatloaf with soybeans and peanuts, long before it became widespread.

"Chris still remembers Montessori's sandpaper letters I made for you. I didn't make much more than that, but you certainly could. Are you thinking about something in particular?"

"Some of Sam's preschool curriculum is supposedly based on her theories," I told Mom. "But he has been on a plateau in his development for a while. I want to do more for him. I just can't depend on the school program to get him caught up to where he needs to be."

Sam didn't refer to himself as "I." Occasionally, he called girls "he" and boys "she." Other parents might appreciate a day off from their toddler's endless questions, but Sam didn't ask them. I wanted Sam to ask people conversation-stopping questions.

"Maria Montessori believed that children learned through their senses," Mom said. "You might just read her books and see what more you can find."

I found some English translations of Maria Montessori's century-old treatises in the downtown library. The pages were yellowed. The books smelled old. No one had checked them out in a long time. I wondered about all the teachers who worked in the half-dozen Montessori schools in Sacramento. Did they learn about her theories in college? Was her life's work reduced to a couple of paragraphs in a textbook on older educational theories? Scanning the text, I soon recognized that she wrote as much a memoir as an educational treatise. She was a medical doctor sent to the Italian ghettos to work with "idiot" children. She soon discovered that the children weren't slow learners at all; the adults were. She observed how children learned: they need order and routine to their learning, they need toys that teach, and they need to experience the world in their way—by seeing, hearing, touching, tasting, and smelling.

I decided to harness Montessori's ideas into activities that would help Sam catch up, but I needed to come up with practical ways to apply her ideas to Sam's needs. I scanned the card catalog for secondary sources, pored over bibliographies, read footnotes for links to real life, and made a lot of phone calls. After a month's time, I had amassed a file drawer full of information, including a book with patterns and directions.

I created a set of vocabulary cards for my first project, thinking that the vocabulary cards the speech therapist used were probably meant to elicit the sound of a letter or a combination of letters. Sam's speech gaps were not simple articulation problems. *He needs help communicating*, I decided. Montessori was convinced that learning new words helped organize a child's mind. I pulled out several old toy catalogs and cut out images of toys that Sam already played with. I pasted each image on a four-by-six-inch card. I made a top card with a picture of a collection of toys. I stacked them all together with a rubber band around them and put them in a plastic, self-clamping box.

"Come on, Sam, let's look at some toys."

I invited him to a spot warmed by the sun shining through the dining room window spilling over the oak floor. Ours were divided-light windows held in a metal frame. We opened the center panel for fresh air on warm days. On cool nights, the windows often fogged up after bath time. I sat down cross-legged next to Sam on the floor and opened the box to show him the cards.

"All toys," I said.

I wanted to show him the routine to follow, so that he would take proper care of the cards. First, I pulled off the rubber band and put the top card upside down next to the stack.

"What is this?" I asked, showing Sam the next card.

"Train," he said. I placed it upside down on the top card.

"Trike."

"Book."

"Bubbles."

"Whirlybird!"

"Blocks."

On we went through the dozen cards in the stack. I flipped the pile over and showed him the top card again and said, "and they're all . . ."

"Toys!" he said.

I rebound the cards with the rubber bands, set the stack back in the box, and clamped it shut.

"Want to do it again?" I asked.

Sam popped the clamps and removed the rubber band from the stack of cards himself. He had more dexterity than the school's evaluation team had discerned. I made a note to myself to read more about dexterity and learn how to help him improve.

I made several more sets of vocabulary cards. From toy, garden, and other mail-order catalogs, I made cards for "in the backyard," "clothes," and "in the kitchen." From free stickers that came in the mail with magazine offers, I made "animals" and "bugs."

Because the cards were organized in conceptual groups, Sam figured out that words could equal more than object-equals-noun. I remembered how encouraged Nancy was when Sam used certain verbs, so I made another card category— "doing things"—with pictures of people eating, jogging, or taking a bath. I started making stacks of cards, hoping they would teach abstract ideas. With one stack, "buildings," I wanted Sam to learn that space had meaning, too.

Sam handled two or three sets of cards every week for a month or two. Some days Sam went through all the cards. I didn't push him to do more than he wanted those days that his interest waned after one or two stacks. Sam never asked me to go through the cards with him, but he went through them by himself occasionally. The "toys" were his favorite. He carefully bundled the cards and put them back in the box each time he used them. But Sam used those cards so often that they got scuffed and dog-eared.

The closer we got to our new baby's arrival, the more time Sam spent in the chest-high sandbox we'd built for him from a *Sunset* magazine pattern, or on the swing set a friend had handed down to us, even on chilly winter days. He spent less time sitting on the driveway, with the wagon upside down and spinning its wheels, or running along the fence watching it go by in the corner of his eye. Finally, Sam was showing improvement in simple social skills, now blooming alongside his speech.

Brothers, Sisters, Aunts, Uncles

My arts council job was part-time, but the organization had grown and I knew the group needed someone to devote full-time to its daily business. I'd encouraged patrons to call me at the gallery. But when I wasn't there, our home phone rang with business on days when I tended to grants and other paperwork to avoid interruptions at the gallery. The phone rang with business even on my days off, but I took them anyway.

Long phone calls were the best time to make bubbles. I held the cordless phone to my ear with my right shoulder and mixed up a super-bubble solution of diluted liquid dish detergent and a touch of corn syrup. The recipe gave the bubbles holding power.

I poured the solution an inch deep into my widest fry pan. Sam followed me outside into the backyard with his big, blue bubble-inside-a-bubble-making wand we got at Fowler's Toys.

As I talked on the phone, I dipped and waved. Sam squealed with delight as he chased bubbles around the yard. He giggled when they popped in the almond tree. He stood, fascinated, when the bubbles came to rest on the bottlebrush bush and refused to pop. Making the huge bubbles didn't solve the council's omnipresent money troubles, but it kept me from becoming stressed over them.

With a new baby on the way, I decided to give up the job. I wanted a few months alone with Sam, without the distractions of the telephone ringing or paper moving. I wanted to focus on helping him before my attention turned to a new baby. Besides, the arts council job wasn't what I'd planned for my life. I wanted to get back to creative work, and possible graduate study, not work my way up a management ladder.

The night before the baby was born, I drifted in and out of a light sleep. The sky outside our bedroom window went from

"Now I'm running."

starry black to deep purple to powdery blue. Mark awoke with an inhale and a stretch.

"Hey, how are you?" he asked, brushing a few stray hairs away from my eyes.

"The contractions kept waking me up last night. I really think today's the day. What do you have to do today?" I asked.

"I've got one job this morning and there's that band concert I'm playing for Al at Yuba College tonight."

Al was the trombone professor and band director at the college in Marysville, about fifty miles away. Mark played in a brass quintet with Al and three accomplished amateur musicians who lived around Marysville. He said that sometimes there was more music happening in the quintet than in the orchestra. He agreed to help Al when the college band lost its tuba player for the spring semester.

"I'll make some calls. Somebody should be able to do it."

I was glad Mom was able to come again, and be my *doula*. There was trouble at home. Chris had just left her husband. She and Ronnie moved in temporarily with Mom and Dad. But they were handling it fine, Mom said.

Sam and Mom were taking turns playing Cosmic Osmo on the computer while Mark and I tried to make last-minute arrangements. The phone rang all morning. Mark managed to get a sub for the daytime work, but not for the evening concert.

"I can't stay home and leave Al in the lurch. I'll only be gone a few hours. Since your mom is here, don't you think you'll be okay?"

"I'm sure we'll be all right," I said. The contractions had not diminished, but they hadn't increased either.

The phone rang once again. It was one of my former professors at the Eastman School of Music calling to say I was accepted for further study in the graduate theory program. I was excited to clear that hurdle—I'd dreamed of being a music professor since high school. But I didn't think I could commit for the upcoming long semester. Summer study was possible, but I couldn't explore all my options just then.

"Bob, I'm not sure how much longer I can talk right now. The contractions are about ten minutes apart," I said.

"Well, my goodness. Congratulations! We don't need to be talking about this now. You can call me later," he laughed.

"Thanks, Bob. I'll get back to you."

Mark left about six thirty. By seven o'clock, I was on the floor on my hands and knees in full labor. I tried to tell Mom how to push her fist into the small of my back the way Mark did when Sam was born. But Mom couldn't bring herself to push as hard as I wanted her to.

By nine o'clock the contractions were less than ten minutes apart and getting stronger. Mercifully, Sam had gone to sleep without much trouble. "Mom, I don't feel comfortable waiting for Mark. I'm going to ask Mike next door to take me," I said.

"Okay, I'll send Mark when he gets home," she said.

I picked up the phone and called Mike. Since he and Judy had two boys, I thought taking me to the hospital would be old hat. But I sensed excitement in his voice. "Come over when you're ready," I said. "I've still got to call the hospital. Would you drive our car?"

By the time I hung up with the hospital nurse, Mike was standing in the entryway chatting with Mom. As Mike and I got into the car, I was thankful for the short trip up Interstate 80 and across Alta Arden to the hospital. I didn't want to have a contraction in the car.

"Thanks, Mike, for doing this," I said. "Mark tried to find a sub for the concert he's playing in Marysville. Wouldn't you know that I'd go into labor as soon as he left."

"That's pretty funny. But what are neighbors for? Say, did you know that there's a big storm coming tonight?"

"No, I missed that," I said, looking out the car window at the full moon.

The moon shined brightly enough to light up the peach orchard along the freeway. I admired that tenacious farmer—boxed in by the interstate, a rail line, and the state fairgrounds—who refused to give up his way of life.

Mike continued to chatter about the weather, but his voice became disembodied inside my head. Instinctively, I looked away from the moon. A wave of pain began low in my belly and radiated along each strand of muscle to the small of my back, where it wadded up like a mutated ball of charley horse. I shifted over to my side and moaned.

"Oh, I'm sorry. I guess we really shouldn't try to talk," Mike said.

We got to the hospital before I had another contraction. Just inside the door of the maternity wing, I dropped to my hands and knees. The triage nurse came out from behind the desk. She did a cursory check of my progress, and decided for a moment that I could wait. She balked when I asked for a birthing room.

"There are other women ahead of you in the exam rooms, and they are waiting to be admitted, too," she said.

The hospital had only two home-style rooms, each outfitted with a special bed for labor, delivery, and recovery. The baby stayed in the room, instead of going to the nursery. I wanted to have my second baby in a home-style room. With Sam, I labored in one room, and when he crowned, the nurse pulled up the side of my gurney and rolled me down the hall to another room. I did not want to repeat that disorienting and undignified experience.

I felt another contraction and dropped to the floor again. The nurse looked at me and looked again to the automatic doors. Another woman in labor dropped in. The nurse picked up a phone. "This is maternity. We're going to need some help down here. I've got two in the admitting rooms, one that just walked in, and a multi that's already dilated and on her hands and knees on the floor."

What did multi *mean in medicalese?* I tried to remember. From one of the books I read while pregnant with Sam I remembered *multigravida*—someone who had a baby before. I didn't read any new baby books this time. After Sam, books couldn't tell me anything new about caring for a baby.

I remembered *multi* was the nurse's code to warn her supervisor about the potential for speedy delivery. I looked at the clock. It was just before ten. Mark was on his way home from Marysville. He would get to the hospital before our baby was born, but not by much. That was good for me. I skipped to the front of the line for a birthing room. The nurse turned to me as I picked myself up from the linoleum.

"It gets this way every time we have a full moon, and now we've got a storm on the way. I can tell it's going to be a busy night tonight," she said, helping me settle in the room with comfortable furnishings and soft lights. So different from the first time, I felt calm, and ready for the work ahead.

The nurse pointed Mike to an oversized easy chair covered in a light-gray vinyl. "Dad, we have a chair for you, too," she said to Mike.

Mike could barely look at the nurse. That was my cue.

"This is my next-door neighbor, Mike. He drove me here. My husband is at work and should be here in about an hour. Can Mike stay until he does?"

"Of course," she replied.

Mike looked relieved. When the nurse left, I asked Mike to push his fist in my back when a contraction came. He helped me through a half-dozen contractions before Mark arrived. As Mark and Mike greeted each other, they made small talk that I found funny.

Trying not to laugh, I rolled into another contraction. I faintly heard Mark telling Mike how he called home during intermission and the line was busy. But he knew something was up when he pulled his pickup truck into the driveway and the Subaru wasn't there. Mom met him at the door, he said, and he didn't even go inside. Another contraction started. I didn't feel like laughing anymore.

"Someone needs to get over here and put a fist in my back!" I yelled.

Mike left. Mark dug in. The contractions grew stronger over the next two hours, until they rolled out one on top of the other. After just a few pushes, our new baby was out.

"It's a boy!" the doctor cried out.

"A boy?" We asked together, and repeated, "It's a boy!"

We had picked out a girl's name that, to this day, I cannot remember. Two nights before he was born, we had discussed boys' names. We had tossed around Paul, but didn't settle on it. I told Mark that if the baby was a boy, we couldn't name him Michael. "If we visit my Aunt Nancy's and everyone in her family was there, and you called out 'Michael,' too many people would think you were calling for them," I said. "My uncle—Mom and Nancy's baby brother—is named Michael. Nancy named her son Michael. And two of her three daughters married men named Michael. You can bet there will be a Michael Jr. in there someday. We absolutely cannot name our baby boy Michael."

Born about one thirty in the morning, our new son looked in much better shape than Sam did as a newborn. He weighed fifteen ounces more. Since my water didn't break until the first push, he had a perfectly round head—a sharp contrast to Sam's head as he was coming out. I hadn't seen it, but Mark said Sam's head was so squished that he looked like the Conehead characters on *Saturday Night Live.*

"I'm hungry," Mark said. "Let's have a party. I'll go get some take-out food."

I tried to doze while Mark was gone. But I was so excited and happy that I couldn't. Our baby was calm and quiet. The nurse brought him back from his first checkup in a bassinet with a humidifier that oozed a warm, mist-filled air through tiny holes in the clear crib walls. When the nurse returned a few minutes later, he cried out to her like a kitten. "Mew," she echoed back.

After the nurse left, I lifted him out of the bassinet and set him on my bed. Mark returned with an icy soda and a crisp white bag filled with cheeseburgers, onion rings, and french fries from a fast-food restaurant. "It was the only place open," he said. I took a few bites.

"I'll wait for the hospital food," I said, pausing for a second, thinking about how Mike had come to the rescue. "We have to name the baby Michael, you know."

"Yeah, I was thinking about that in the car. How about Michael Jacob? You know, for Jake."

Jake was one of Mark's many mentors, the principal tuba player with the Chicago Symphony.

"I like that." I took out the birth certificate papers and began to fill in the blanks. First name, Michael—the archangel, Christ's performer on earth, I remembered. Middle name, Jacob—the second son of Isaac.

"Hey, you should check out the misty air in that bassinet," I motioned.

Mark walked over to the crib and touched the cotton bedding.

"That feels fantastic! I want to crawl in there myself. Why don't they make something like that for adults?" he asked.

He came back to the bed to pick up Michael.

"Hey, little buddy, you smell good. You smell all sweet, like your mom."

Our birthday party lasted about long enough for Mark to eat his cheeseburger and fries. He fell asleep in the easy chair as soon as he put Michael back in bed with me. He woke up at dawn and went home to change clothes.

Mark brought Mom and Sam back with him. Sam warmed to Michael right away. He touched Michael's fingers and poked gently at his eyelids. He took off Michael's blue cotton cap and put his hand over the top of Michael's head, feeling Michael's pulse through his soft spot. *How did he know to do that?* I wondered. He put his cheek to Michael's head to feel it.

I wasn't worried that Sam would ever intentionally hurt Michael. But I did wonder if Sam would notice that a baby brother was different than, say, a dog. Now, watching the two of them, I realized that was silly.

After returning home from the hospital, I was up most of the night, rocking in the platform rocker in our bedroom and nursing Michael. I watched the rain out our window, pouring down on our neighbor's palm trees, washing the sidewalks and making gentle streams in the street. Michael nursed, slept, and nursed again, until my milk finally came in about four o'clock in the morning.

"You're a hungry fellow, aren't you?" I said, while Mark snored in the bed.

I wasn't tired. The steady rain was a stalwart friend. Just as the weather people predicted, the storm brought the end of the drought. They called it the "March Miracle." I looked at our quiet, content baby with his ten tiny fingers and ten tiny toes. He was normal.

For now, that was enough.

Summer Vacations

MARK AND I VACILLATED OVER WHETHER we could afford to spend two long semesters in Rochester. Summer school seemed feasible. Either way, we'd need more money in the bank. I applied to the state arts agency and a nonprofit arts advocacy group. I made some calls and waited to see where my job hunt would take me.

Juggling a baby and a busy preschooler wasn't as taxing as I feared. Michael was a curious baby. He didn't cry the way Sam did as an infant. He slept easily, and for long stretches at a time. With his hearty appetite, he grew fast. He nursed on both sides, making breastfeeding easy and comfortable. *Such a thing to find comfort in*, I thought.

Michael took his morning nap while Sam was in school. I relished the few quiet hours to myself. I cleaned the house and finished some long-neglected sewing and gardening projects. Our backyard almost looked good enough to be featured in a gardening magazine, which encouraged us to spend even more time outside with the boys.

The previous homeowner, a woman who raised a daughter in the house and lived in it until she died, had filled the backyard

"I threw rocks in the river because I wanted to make a splash."

with a wide variety of trees and flowering bushes. But like the house, the garden had been neglected for several years before we moved in. I cut back the jungle of branches and vines. I pulled many weeds to uncover the woman's antique rose bush with its large, rich, red blooms. The Valencia orange tree, in one corner, and the Meyer lemon bush in the other, looked good with just a little pruning. Some of the overgrown vines on the patio's south side couldn't be tamed with the pruning shears. Mark helped me pull them out. He replaced them with one of his favorites, a fragrant purple wisteria that quickly covered the arbor over the patio until it reached the Japanese maple that shaded the north side.

He had to dig for two days to remove the stump of a dead tree left in the center of the backyard. In its place, I planted a self-pollinating almond tree. The tree grew vigorously. We enjoyed its early spring bloom, although it would take a few years for the big yields to come in.

I didn't have such good luck with a pair of grapevines I planted behind the swing set. The grapes came in green and seedy each year, but I couldn't figure out what went wrong. Since the vines were pretty, I left them alone.

After I pulled weeds around the raspberries, they spread along the fence. Those sweet rubies kept producing until almost Christmas. Before breakfast, I liked to go out in my red silk sleep shirt, barefoot, and eat the ripe ones off their canes.

On Sam's last day of preschool for the year, I strapped Michael into the car and drove the two-mile route to campus to pick Sam up at noon, just as we did every day. Sam wasn't patient enough to spend thirty long minutes riding a meandering bus route that didn't bring him straight home for lunch. Today, though, Sam was slow in putting his blocks away. Mrs. Vargas stayed behind with Sam as the teacher's aide took the other boys to the bus. She wanted to tell me about Sam's progress over the past few months.

"I've really enjoyed having Sam in my class," Mrs. Vargas said. "He still paces during circle time, but he tries to sit with the others. Even though he isn't in a summer program, you can read to him. You can also encourage him to write his letters and numbers so he doesn't regress."

That meant no lazy days tubing in secret swimming holes, no laughing through silly children's theater, no dancing along with concerts in the park. Mrs. Vargas had other ideas for Sam. I appreciated her recommendations. But outside was a fragrant, sunny late-spring day. I had visions of going to the new playground in Davis, lying down with a good book atop a thick flannel blanket. Michael would nap. Sam would explore the playground's elaborate pattern of slides, turrets, and tunnels. Running through them must have felt like being in an Escher painting. An architect had designed it, just like many other playgrounds like it across the nation. The kids told him what they wanted, and parents and other volunteers built the playground in a weekend or two.

As Mrs. Vargas and I left the classroom, Sam ran down the hall to the front door. With Michael on my hip, I couldn't chase him down anymore. Unlike other kids his age, Sam never turned back to see whether I was watching. Where was his instinct to stay close to his family, or his teacher, or whoever was caring for him?

I worried that Sam would run too far one day. He roamed fearlessly. Once—a month or so before Michael was born—I left Sam to play alone in the living room. Mark needed help with a computer problem in our makeshift office at the back of the kitchen. While I was out of the room, Sam let himself out the front door for a walk. I came back in the living room ten or fifteen minutes later, startled to see a young woman coming up our front steps with Sam.

"Your son seems to know where he lives," she had said with this searching, frightened look in her eyes.

"I found him near Stockton Boulevard."

After she left, I waited for the other shoe to drop—perhaps a call or visit from the child protection agency—but it didn't happen.

Mrs. Vargas never mentioned whether Sam had bolted away from her or the other teachers. Carrying, and caring for, Michael forced my perceived safety net around Sam to expand. I learned the past few months that I could trust Sam to wait for me, that he had developed his own internal governor.

As we neared the door, Mrs. Vargas turned to me and asked, "Did you ever think Sam might have autism?"

"Autism?"

The word set thoughts swirling in my mind. Mrs. Vargas said something after asking the question, but I wasn't listening. I remembered that I had heard the word once or twice before. Dustin Hoffman won an Oscar for playing a man with autism. But I couldn't remember the name of the film or much about the autistic character. The son of a doctor on the television show *St. Elsewhere* had autism. I'd seen the show a few times. The doctor's son sat in the corner of his room and rocked back and forth. He talked nonsensically to his sister. He banged his head on the wall. He jumped on the bed. Tommy, that was the character's name. The same as in *Tommy*, a rock opera by the Who.

Now, why was that name stuck in my ear? I wondered. *"He ain't got no distractions, can't hear those buzzers an' bells. Don't see no lights a-flashin', plays by sense of smell." That wasn't Sam. What on earth was Mrs. Vargas thinking?*

"Well, I shouldn't have even mentioned it." Mrs. Vargas backtracked as my eyes refocused on her face.

Michael picked up on the tension. He began to fuss and squirm. Sam whined.

"We'd better go," I said.

"Really, thinking about it, no. I don't think so. It's not autism," she said.

Mrs. Vargas violated the Rules by labeling my child. That much I knew. But in the past few years, I had learned to trust my moments of clarity. I wondered if I shouldn't trust hers, too. After all, she had spent five mornings a week with Sam. It took courage to share her instincts with me, especially when she knew she could be reprimanded for doing so.

We said our good-byes. I helped Sam push open the front door of the school building, and we headed toward the car. Sam ran ahead of Michael and me again. When I caught up, I opened the back door of the sedan. Sam crawled in and helped buckle Michael into his old car seat. He waited for me to dig his own seat buckle out of the crack between the cushions. I handed Sam the buckle and watched him snap himself into his booster seat. As I walked around to the driver's side, I told myself that if Mrs. Vargas changed her mind about autism, I didn't need to worry about it anymore.

Sam didn't sit in a corner and rock away the hours singing a meaningless mantra like that boy on *St. Elsewhere*. He did speak with an odd inflection, however, as if English weren't his native tongue. His vocabulary was unsophisticated. But it had expanded with our intervention. I turned the ignition key and reminded myself that Sam was bright. Everyone who had examined Sam told us so. As I pulled away from the school, I wondered why no one in the world had yet invented a test to measure Sam's intelligence.

When Mark came home to eat between two rehearsals, I recapped the conversation with Mrs. Vargas. I could tell the word surprised him, too.

"Right after she said it, she denied it," I said. "I don't get it."

Mark considered the confusion for a moment.

"I think we've been pushing him pretty hard," he said. "Maybe we shouldn't put him in another special education class. Maybe if we just leave him alone for a while, he'll find his own way."

I remembered how hard it was for Sam to sit in groups and to keep up with the increasingly elaborate play schemes. He seemed to be at his best in one-on-one situations, with adults.

"You could be right. Sam's preschool program hasn't helped him as much as I hoped. The teacher has them do so much in groups," I said. "You know, I've been thinking. Maybe we should see if we can enroll him at a Montessori school. They supposedly let kids go at their own pace and toward their own interests. They call it child-directed learning."

"I'd feel a lot more comfortable with that," Mark replied.

"Maybe we can start visiting schools over the summer," I said.

I drifted back to the kitchen office, pulled the yellow pages out from under a pile of papers, and began looking up numbers of private schools. We'd gotten by on Mark's tuba and personnel manager salaries. Private school would be expensive. I needed to push a little harder on my job search. I also needed to find a place for this word that had finally surfaced, like a bit of gold washed out during a Sierra rainstorm, floating downstream, waiting to be claimed.

Potty Training

I liked Ken and Jennifer, co-workers at my new job at the California Confederation of the Arts. They were good-hearted people, dedicated to the group's mission of promoting the arts. Both Ken, my boss, and Susan, the executive director, prided themselves on their family-friendly office policies. They encouraged Mark to bring Michael to the office to nurse during my first few weeks on the job. My body needed to adjust to routine feedings, instead of breastfeeding on demand. Within a month, Michael and I lined up with morning, noon and evenings feedings and Mark didn't have to bring him anymore. Instead, I bicycled home at noon to share lunch with Mark and Sam, and nurse Michael.

Before moving to Texas, the Confederation's outgoing office manager, Blair, trained me to do her job. Blair motored around the office in her wheelchair. I wondered if Ken built the ramp from the parking lot to the back door for her, since the front door emptied onto the sidewalk on P Street, near the capitol. Blair told me how, as a teenager, she was paralyzed from the waist down after an illness. She still had enough feeling in her legs that she had hope she could walk again. If she lived with her family, she would have more support to build her strength. Later, Jennifer told me that she doubted Blair's ambition. Jennifer thought the push to walk again was coming from Blair's family. I listened to Jennifer's doubts and began to wonder, if it takes all the energy you have to walk and you have none left for your other daily tasks, then what have you accomplished?

After the California Assembly started proposing cuts for its arts funding statewide, Jennifer, Ken, and I began notifying the group's elaborate network of advocates. We sent fax alerts out

"I liked the bubble bath."

and activated phone trees. The three of us working in the tiny P Street office were deluged. One Friday, in the thick of the legislative session, Susan called a strategy meeting at her home office in San Francisco. We needed to brainstorm with several public relations and lobbying consultants. I figured the meeting would end after lunch, so I persuaded Mark to bring the family into the city for a day trip.

When Sam was almost two, the Loma Prieta earthquake had destroyed a section of the Bay Bridge, bringing an end to our occasional day trips into San Francisco. We'd found cheap ways to amuse ourselves in the city. We liked testing the hillholder brakes on our car, and getting that roller-coaster feeling from rounding the tops of the steep hills and weaving down Lombard Street's brick-topped hairpin turns. We ate sourdough bread and soup from vendors along Fisherman's Wharf. We strolled with the pigeons and the homeless in Union Square Park. Michael's calm disposition gave us confidence to take the boys window-shopping at the big upscale toy stores near the park. I loved the fabric store in the skinny building on Geary Street. It was four stories high, with the first three stuffed from floor to ceiling with colors, weaves, and fibers. The fourth was stuffed with buttons, notions, and ribbons. I could wander in that store for hours. But I didn't want to try the patience of Mark and the boys.

Early in the afternoon, Sam told us he needed to go to the bathroom. Mark took him to a public restroom, but Sam refused to go. Sam had learned to use the potty at home, but he never went to the bathroom at school. This was his first trip to a public men's room. *Maybe Sam just needs to feel safe*, I thought. I took him into the ladies' room with me. He still refused to pee.

"Maybe he needs to go in a home bathroom," I said to Mark.

"Where are we going to find that in Union Square?" Mark shot back. Sam had to go. He'd be yelling soon.

"We could go back to Susan's," I said, even though hers was the last bathroom in San Francisco I wanted to take Sam to.

When we appeared at Susan's front door, Sam was screaming in discomfort. "Of course, of course, come in," Susan and her husband said sympathetically. Mark offered a perfunctory greeting and pushed Sam into their bathroom. Sam's screams grew louder still. Over the din, Susan and her husband told us they felt badly for Sam. They also came up with ideas that might encourage Sam to pee. But Sam refused to use their toilet, too.

Mark and I left Susan's with a screaming three-and-a-half-year-old, a crying baby, and a new low in levels of humiliation. The trip home would be two hours long if the traffic flowed. I silently prayed for Sam to have an accident, just to end his endless screaming. Oddly, once Michael was tucked into his car seat, he wasn't upset by the ordeal. He apparently was accustomed to Sam's screaming.

On the long drive home, I put two fingers inside my ears when I could. I recalled a similar incident, when Sam was eighteen months old. He'd held his poop for a week. Mark called me at the gallery to tell me that Sam wouldn't get out of bed, that he was lying on his belly crying. Mark said Sam couldn't get up and he couldn't bear to lie on his back. Mark had managed to feel some spots in his lower belly that were hard as stone. When I got home, we took Sam to the pediatric clinic and got the bare-light-bulb treatment from the doctor on duty.

The doctor felt Sam's belly and he whined and whimpered all the while.

"We usually don't see this sort of thing unless parents are potty training," he had said, looking at me. I studied his piercing gaze. I was convinced that, if I argued with him at all, I would only confirm his suspicion that I had caused all this.

"Are you sure you're not pushing him?" the doctor asked.

Blood rushed to my ears.

"No," Mark weighed in. "I don't know how he got to this point, but I think he's scared of going at all now."

I exhaled. The doctor left for a few minutes.

"Thanks for that, honey," I told Mark. "It seemed like he'd already made up his mind about me."

"Yeah. Well, he was wrong," Mark said.

The doctor returned a minute later and handed Mark some latex gloves and samples of water-based lubricant.

"Better if one of you does it, so he won't be as traumatized," he advised.

Now, listening to Sam's screams again, I began to wonder about the advice we were getting from the so-called experts in their chosen field. I knew Sam's behavior wasn't normal. But I also learned this past year that asking the experts about things that didn't seem normal only brought upon us more, stupid-young-parent admonishments.

Mark turned the car into the driveway. I stepped out and ran to unlock the house. Sam unbuckled himself, dashed into the bathroom, sat down on his white plastic potty chair that looked like a miniature toilet, and let go.

Peace and relief at last, I thought, sitting on the top of the big toilet next to Sam's.

Mark caught up and stood in the bathroom doorway, holding Michael.

"I can't believe he did that," he said. "I can't believe he held it that long just to go in that goddamn potty."

I looked at the two of them in the doorway, and back at the square pink tiles that lined the shower walls around the tub. I studied the old chrome fixtures with their calcified buildup around the joints. When we first moved in, I remembered how the buildup on the old glass shower doors was so bad that we junked the doors to hang cheery, pink shower curtains instead. A brown plastic basket of bath toys sat in the back of the dry tub. One set of toys was the three fat men of the Mother Goose rhyme that floated merrily, but in boats that looked like a green turtle, red boat, and blue pitcher. There was a faded, red-and-yellow plastic watering can and several nesting cups, too.

Sam knew how to push the cups, upside down, straight to the bottom of the tub to release big, noisy bubbles. That always made Michael giggle, though it was clear that making Michael giggle was not Sam's prime motivation for making bubbles. There were also windup toys that swam. Nancy encouraged us to buy the windup toys because they helped develop Sam's dexterity and taught him about cause and effect.

I smiled, thinking about how much Sam enjoyed bath time.

"We'll take the potty chair with us next time we take a trip," I said, looking up at Mark.

"I feel stupid for not thinking of it before," he replied.

After that day, if we headed down the street and forgot the potty chair, we went back to the house to get it.

A New Home!

The Sacramento Symphony's season ended with yet another deficit. The symphony association board was borrowing heavily against its small endowment and other assets in order to make each month's payroll. With so many other orchestras going bankrupt elsewhere in California and around the country, Mark was terrified. He doubted his job would last much longer.

"That's the old Macintosh computer we had. I used to play Cosmic Osmo."

"If they go under, this may be the last job I ever have," Mark said.

"Maybe a year off would help," I said. "Why not ask for a sabbatical? The quality of music-making in Rochester is inspiring. You can hang around the apartment with the boys and practice as much as you want."

We talked about Mark's career and concluded that a sabbatical from the orchestra and a year in New York would be a wise investment in Mark's future. He could practice for auditions for other jobs. We decided it best to go to New York now, rather than in a year or two, when it could get riskier financially.

I reluctantly left my new job. We found a young couple to rent our home for a year, and secured a flat in the graduate-student housing at the University of Rochester. What didn't fit in the Subaru sedan, the back of the Isuzu pickup, or the rented trailer from U-Haul, we stored in our garage.

We left Sacramento in the scorching heat of late summer, and headed across the country toward upstate New York. The trip took only a few days. Arriving in Rochester in early September, crisp autumn breezes already seasoned the air. The night we arrived, a man who identified himself in a thick Cantonese accent as our neighbor helped us move our belongings inside our flat. After that night, we never saw the man again, although we tried looking for him to say thanks. I called him our "moving angel."

Our building resembled the dozens of other old, well-kept two-story brick- and wood-sided buildings dotting the greens on the south side of the University of Rochester's River Campus. Our flat was upstairs. That meant an entire stairwell stood between us and the heavy storm doors that held back winter's icy air. On sunny days, the rays of light flooded the living room floor and ran up the walls. Even on cloudy days, our south-facing windows imparted a warm glow in the big room that we furnished sparsely. We put the platform rocker in one corner of the room. Opposite the windows, we put our imported pine bookshelves. In addition to storing books and records, we used the shelves to record the boys' growth by measuring their heights and etching them, along with the date, on the side panel. We unrolled the maroon-and-black Arabian rug Dad bought for us in Riyadh to make a warm spot on the hard oak floor.

Mark and I put our bed, and a forest of tubas, in the bigger bedroom and set up the other bedroom with a twin bed for Sam and the portable crib for Michael. I brought several buckets of toys, carefully selected to encourage Sam's play. I also brought the art easel I built for Sam with Dad's help. Looking at the easel, I remembered that last Christmas Eve I was sanding the wood madly in Dad's woodshop, trying to finish the easel, a Christmas present for Sam.

A few nights after our arrival, Sam shattered one pane in his bedroom window. We had no idea how he did it, since we didn't hear anything other than the sound of shattering glass. When we asked him what happened, he couldn't tell us. Mark taped some cardboard over the hole to keep out the cold and in the morning, he went to the hardware store and replaced the shattered glass.

Michael was crawling now. Since we weren't sure what either boy would do at the top of a stairwell, we put a safety gate on the doorway to the landing. Mark and I could easily hurdle the white-and-gray plastic grid—a minor inconvenience to keep the boys safe.

We brought along our custom tandem bicycle and I bought another stump-jumping bike to ride around campus. I taught a section of beginning music theory classes as a teaching assistant at the University of Rochester. Even on winter days, the roads and bikeways were often clear and dry enough to ride the three-mile path along the Genesee River all the way to my graduate classes downtown. When the roads were wet or covered with snow, I rode the university's big blue shuttle bus.

Each day when I got home from school, I opened the door and wheeled the bicycle inside to park it at the bottom of the stairwell. Sam leaned out over the safety gate and looked down at me with a beaming smile. "Mom's home!" he would exclaim.

"Mom's home!" Mark would always echo from somewhere else upstairs.

The first time Sam did that, I realized that I had waited a long time for such an expression of love from him. Then I realized I didn't even know I was waiting for it. The details of the moment flooded my senses: the glow of sunlight oozing from behind him on the landing, the reverberation of his voice in the stairwell, the sparkle of his toothy smile. His affection tumbled down the stairs and welled up in my eyes.

"Hi, Sam!" I yelled back.

Each day, when I came home and Sam exclaimed, "Mom's home!" my heart felt just a little lighter inside my chest.

Favorite Foods

While running around the Eastman School of Music the first week, Mark and I bumped into Bob in the elevator. We told him we were looking for a preschool for Sam. He told us how his children had thrived with Patti Salata. She taught an old-fashioned nursery school on weekday mornings in a neighborhood church basement.

"I liked to sleep a lot."

The half-dozen children in Patti's little nursery school all sat around a giant picnic table. On any given day, the children did simple things like sculpt with salt dough and smear gooey finger paint in primary colors over manila paper. The children took turns going down a two-foot plastic slide, clapping for each other. Patti read children's books by Margaret Wise Brown and sang to them to teach them finger plays. Her gentle, mellow manner and teaching methods contrasted with the more intense play stations at parent-participation preschool in Sacramento.

Sam enjoyed Patti's nursery school and quickly became attached to the other children. He would talk about them at home.

"Nathan's sick today," he said one day.

"Michele got a band-aid," he said on another.

After many months of worry about Sam's development, we began to relax. Sam was doing fine. Maybe California's fast-paced approach to early education wasn't suited to him.

Early one afternoon, the phone rang. It was Patti. She needed to talk to me, she said. I could tell that she was nervous. I grew terrified. With the cordless phone pinned between my shoulder and my ear, I stepped over the safety gate and sat down at the top of the landing. A cool draft wafted up from the bottom of the stairs, yet sweat was seeping out my face and palms. Maybe another child's parent complained about Sam after school today. Maybe she's going to ask us to pull Sam out of her little group.

My mind was racing, careening around corners. Surely, Patti had grown attached to Sam these past few weeks, too. Surely, she knew that he responded to her warmth. I should have let her know how much more Sam responded to her than to his other teachers in California.

Slowly my mind focused back on Patti and the stammering in her voice.

"So, I wondered if you'd ever taken him to anyone to be evaluated because it just seems to me that Sam might have autism," she said.

Patti inhaled as she waited for my reply.

"Funny you should say that," I said, racing to cover any trace of my inattention. "We had Sam in a special ed program in California to help his speech." I prattled on about Sam's schooling and therapy up until now. I was greatly relieved that she didn't ask us to pull him from her class. Worry crept back in. Maybe she planned on asking for that next? And why was I not shocked to hear the word *autism* again?

"Sam's last teacher suggested he had autism. At least, she said so once, but she wasn't sure. Frankly, I don't really know what autism looks like. We were trying so hard to help him last year, pushing him so hard. After a while, we didn't think he was making any progress. We decided to be a little more low-key and see what he does on his own."

I hoped Patti understood—our ideas, our hopes, our fears. All of it.

"I thought I should say something," Patti said. "There are people here who can help. But if you still want to keep him with me in nursery school, I'm happy to have him."

I exhaled again. I felt like Sam made considerable progress with Patti because she wasn't trying to accomplish specific remedial or educational goals. Patti's little nursery school was about enjoying childhood activities.

"I can't say that we won't be thinking about this autism thing, especially since you aren't the first one to bring it up," I said.

I wanted her to know that I appreciated her courage. "And I'm glad you'll still have him. We don't have any wild expectations. Like I said, this year, we just wanted to leave him alone."

We both exhaled and said our goodbyes.

"That was Patti on the phone," I told Mark.

"Was there some kind of problem with Sam in school?"

"She thinks he might have autism," I said.

"Did you tell her about last year? Did you tell her what Mrs. Vargas said?" Mark said, before panicking. "Wait a minute, did she say that she doesn't want him in her preschool anymore?"

"I told her we purposely didn't want to do anything special, that we wanted to leave Sam alone this year and see how he'd do on his own. Don't worry. She said she'll still have him."

Mark returned to slicing fruit for Michael and setting it on his high-chair tray. Sam had just finished with his lunchtime bowl of cereal and trotted into the living room to play with his wooden train.

Sam consumed cold breakfast cereal morning, noon, and night now. He was willing to eat a variety of cereals, including those that had dried fruit or nuts. I fortified the milk with extra protein and beneficial bacteria, and gave both Sam and Michael daily multivitamins. It worried me that his diet was so limited, but he hadn't had a vomiting episode since we moved to Rochester. I didn't know if it was because he only ate cereal, or because the water was cleaner here, or something else altogether. It bothered me the most that I didn't know why.

Before we moved to Rochester, Sam had whittled his food choices week by week over the course of a year. First he refused his breakfast shakes, then fruit. He stopped eating whole-wheat pancakes after I didn't cook one pancake long enough. Sam gagged on a bit of runny batter in the middle and pushed the plate away. After that, he refused pancakes, waffles, and french toast. Guilt by association, I figured.

Sam stopped eating most everything else after he threw it up. It happened so often that we got to know the pattern, from his piercing howl in the middle of the night to the way he ate his meals the day before. I'd mentioned the pattern—how, at least once a month, he would gorge himself during the day and vomit in the middle of the night—to Sam's pediatrician. She listened to my careful description of Sam's food trauma. She mumbled something about kids getting sick occasionally, and followed that with a blank stare.

How many times had I gotten that stare? How many times had my observations been dismissed, or simply ignored? We were swimming in the open ocean and our baby's life depended on us knowing the right way to go. She was no more help than any of the others. I could only imagine what she might be thinking. Did she think my kitchen was filthy? Did she think I fed my family rotten food?

The last time Sam threw up we'd had one of our best family meals, a traditional Japanese recipe I taught myself. I learned to transform pork, rice, and cabbage into the same savory combination I'd tasted when my friend Masako took me to her favorite *tonkatsu* shop in Tokyo.

That night, Mark and I set up our dinner on the coffee table in the living room, in the Japanese tradition, and sat on the floor to watch a baseball game. Sam didn't eat the finely shredded cabbage, but he quickly ate the spoonful of rice and tonkatsu pieces we put on his plate. He helped himself to the extra pieces on the platter, bite after ravenous bite. Watching our three-year-old boy devour more than the two of us combined, we looked helplessly at each other. Mark picked up the platter and took it back to the kitchen. We both dreaded what might happen later.

About three o'clock in the morning, Sam woke with a howl. We rushed to his room and turned on the lights. He turned to us, his face screwed tight with pain and his brown eyes vacant. Stiffly, he tried to push himself up from his pillow. His howls stopped as suddenly as they started. I managed to get a towel between him and his bedding before he heaved. Out came dinner. He heaved again and again. Out came lunch, out came breakfast. Chewed, but not digested.

When Sam's belly was empty, Mark picked him up and took him to the bathroom. Mark carefully peeled away Sam's pajamas so as not to soil him further. With his big, callused hands, he tenderly washed Sam's hands and face over the sink.

Something was terribly wrong with Sam, maybe something degenerative. No one was helping us. We knew nothing to do to fix it.

But I can keep him clean, I thought.

I went back to Sam's bedroom and carefully pulled the sheets, pillowcase, and mattress pad from his bed. I took them, along with the towel and pajamas, to the washing machine.

I made up Sam's bed with clean linens while Mark slowly rocked our baby in the platform rocker that we'd bought at a secondhand furniture store before he was born. Sam fell asleep in Mark's arms. I turned out the light as Mark tucked Sam under clean covers with a kiss and a tiny toss of his hair.

The next morning, I took the pajamas and linens outside to dry and disinfect in the sunlight. I fanned the creases out of the sheets. The sun felt soothing and warm on my face and chest.

I folded each sheet in half and pinned it to the line from my small pocketful of wood clothespins. As I pinned up the pillowcase, pad, towel, and pajamas, I breathed in the soft fragrance of the honeysuckle growing over the back stoop.

Gentle breezes stirred the line. The laundry was crisp and clean-smelling by afternoon. Piece by piece, I took it down and folded it all neatly into the laundry basket, except the fitted sheet, which I never have been able to fold flat.

I stacked the fresh linens back in the closet and returned Sam's pajamas to his dresser drawer, blinking back tears.

Baby's Outings

By the time autumn had kissed the tops of the sugar maples and the red oak trees, we felt at home in upstate New York.

"Any afternoon without rain and above fifty-five degrees is fair bike-riding weather, as far as I'm concerned," Mark said, conceding that our biking days in balmy California had become a distant memory. No matter how many hours of study I had ahead of me, I knew I'd think better after a bike ride. Some days in graduate school, I felt like I imagined Sam must feel every day in preschool—markedly ahead of fellow students in some things, unbearably behind in others.

I often dashed home after my classes for an hour-long ride in the late afternoon with Mark and the boys. We bundled them up with hats, helmets, coats, and mittens. We covered them with flannel blankets in the yellow and red trailer hooked up to the back of our tandem bicycle. Most people seemed to enjoy the strange sight of our motley bicycle crew. They'd wave and we'd wave back. As our captain, though, Mark had to keep his focus on the trail. As stoker, it was my job to balance the bike and pedal hard, especially when the hills got high.

The boys loved to bounce along the bike trail that followed the Erie Canal. We pedaled by people walking, jogging, and trying out rollerblades. We saw small boats in the canal from time to time. One Saturday, a small leisure boat was negotiating the locks and we stopped for a long time to watch it. I was pleased to see the boys' patience and curiosity as we watched the locks fill and drain, fold and unfold.

"Now that's goofy. I used to ride with Michael
in a trailer pulled by Mom and Dad's bike."

We discovered wild apple trees along the route. When the fruit began to fall, we tucked a brown paper bag in the back of the trailer so we could stop and pick the best ones. Back at the flat, I made a tangy applesauce with cinnamon. Sam wouldn't touch it, but Michael enjoyed it.

The trail was paved close to town. But further out, past Penfield, it was covered with fine gravel. On wet days we turned around at the gravel. If we didn't, the mud sprayed up and off the back tire and stuck to the back of my jacket, or up the front of the trailer. The boys thought the mud spray was hysterically funny.

One dry day we made it all the way to Fairfield where there was a store like Fowler's, with toys packed from floor to ceiling. Another day, Mark drove too slowly down a curb by the Jewish Community Center and the tandem twisted perilously sideways. I felt the bike tipping, and I planted my left foot down to try to stop it from falling. Suddenly, and quite forcefully, the handlebars pulled out of my grip.

As the bike dropped beneath me, I looked back over my shoulder to see the trailer hook turn sideways with the tandem. The boys were safe inside, but giggling uncontrollably at Mark who continued to tumble to the pavement with the bike and just lay there, laughing.

Baby's Birthdays

For Sam's fourth birthday, we gave him a fresh set of watercolors and crisp, white paper. Once, Sam drew a face with a dark, brown crayon on kraft paper, but otherwise he liked to paint dripping rainbow segments on the easel I made for him. The segments mimicked the light fragments cast on the boys'

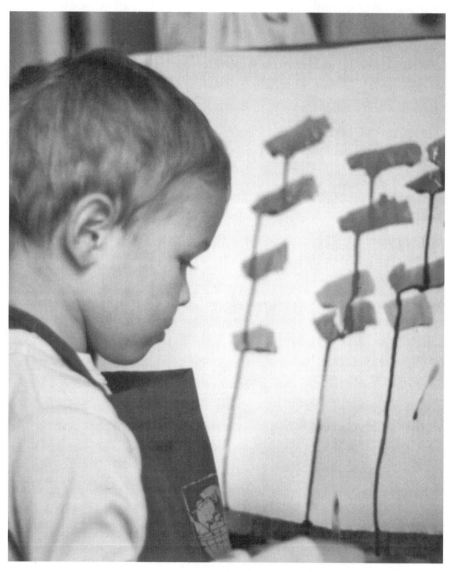

"I used to enjoy painting. This is a rainbow."

bedroom wall by a small prism we'd put in the window. Sam painted so many rainbow segments that we bought a tray of watercolors every week at Wegmans grocery store. I often resorted to cutting the paper sacks in half to insure he had enough paper to paint on.

I earned better grades on my first-term graduate exams than I expected, yet I still felt out of step with the other students. Mark and I decided to spend Christmas break in Colorado with my family. I planned to spend some vacation time researching and reading about autism.

For a small-town library, Windsor's was well-stocked. I picked out several books that looked promising, including *Autism: Explaining the Enigma* by Uta Frith.

The book's well-preserved cover featured a print of the famous seventeenth-century painting by Georges de la Tour, *The Cheat with the Ace of Diamonds*. I opened the book back at my parents' house, skipping the acknowledgements and diving into chapter one. Frith made her case with another mother's words that read as if I were writing about my own child: *"'She was so pretty—hazel eyes with long curling eyelashes and finely tapered eyebrows, flaxen coloured curls and such a sweet, far-away expression; I hoped against hope that all would eventually go well, and that she was just a slow starter.'"*

I turned halfway down the next page. Frith drew a composite sketch of a boy named Peter.

"In photographs he looks a handsome, healthy, and happy baby. . . ."

I could feel my heart beating through my temples. This boy resonated so loudly in my head. The images of *St. Elsewhere*'s Tommy weren't autism. Peter—this was autism—a boy who loved his family, but didn't talk *with* them as much as *at* them. He didn't play with army men or put on puppet shows, or use his plastic dinosaurs to knock down Lincoln Log houses.

"Peter never did anything of the kind. He had a large collection of toy cars, but instead of playing with them in the way his little cousin did, he was interested only in placing them in long straight lines and in closely observing the spinning of the wheels."

My eyes froze on *wheels*. Ronnie handed Sam a five-pound laundry soap bucket full of Matchbox cars when he outgrew the collection. *That is how Sam plays with them!* I closed the book and sprang up, startling Mom.

"He's got it. It's right there in that book. I just read it. He's just like that kid, Peter, in the book. Sam's got autism."

Mark looked at me with vacant eyes. I walked back to the guest room, leaving the book behind. I wanted to read on. I knew I needed more of the story than those few pages of the first chapter. But that was as far as I could go for now. Mark drifted away from the table and my peripheral vision. But I saw Mom reach for the book and struggle to focus as she turned pages.

I sat on the guest room floor. I originally planned on leaving the boys' clothes in the suitcase for the summer. Mom offered us closet space to hang things, but she didn't have any drawer space. The dressers that used to be filled with my and my sisters' clothes were now filled with neatly folded scraps of material and dress patterns, ribbons and rolls of wrapping paper. But, one by one, I took the boys' clothes out of the suitcase, sorted and refolded them, putting them in little piles along the bedroom wall.

I looked up to see Mom standing in the doorway. I could tell she was having a hard time watching me. Looking at her, I was certain that she never aged, at least, until I saw old photos, when Chris, Karen, Teresa and I were little and she was young and looked like Jackie Kennedy.

She looked hurt and worried. I started to cry.

"Imagining what Sam's life will be, I don't even know what to think now. I never imagined that he wouldn't fall in love, or get married and have kids of his own," I said. I was saying things I didn't know were in my head. Typically, I thought before I spoke. Words came after thoughts.

"Maybe. But you don't know that for sure," Mom said, still standing in the doorway. "You don't know what the future is. You should talk to Teresa. While she was going to physical therapy school at the University of Utah, Teresa worked with a few children who had autism. Maybe she can help."

"Really? I didn't know that. I wondered Teresa didn't say something before."

Mom turned and left.

I continued to refold the boys' clothes and arrange them in piles. *Breathe in, breathe out*, I coached myself. The tears flowed from somewhere dark and deep. What was this place? I recognized it as the same space where great melodies and harmonies had also swept in many times and washed me away. My head was telling me that Sam needed me to be clearheaded, but my heart was telling me something else altogether. How was I supposed to trust where my emotions were taking me?

I went back to get Frith's book off the table. I settled in Dad's brown leather and chrome recliner and lingered over the next two chapters that traced history and literature for stories of autism. Psychologists had only named it *autism*, or *Asperger's syndrome*, in the 1940s. Frith recounted historic stories of the Wild Boy of Aveyron and Kasper Hauser, drew poetic links in the Grimm fairy tales of Sleeping Beauty and Snow White, and delved into the detail-obsessed Sherlock Holmes. I was touched by Frith's retelling of the tales of Brother Juniper, whose travails both inspired and exasperated his leader, St. Francis of Assisi, and the other members of their spiritual order. Brother Juniper's pure, innocent heart shone through each story. I was struck by how similar Sam was to him, too.

A few days later, I phoned Teresa in Salt Lake City. Once we got to talking about autism and her experiences working with her physical therapy clients, her tone slid from sisterly to professional.

"So, you worked with kids with autism? What was that like?" I asked.

"Well, with this one boy, we just read together. He would read a bit and get up and run around the room," she said. "It took forever to get a page read."

"How old was he?" I asked, hopeful about the reading part, unconcerned about the running-around-the-room part.

"Eight. You should know that most kids with autism don't have much of a chance for an independent life. Only a few are able to live on their own without support."

My baby sister's declaration that most kids with autism don't have much chance for an independent life could have sent me into a tailspin. But it rifled past my ears. Sam as an adult seemed far in the future, and too far to worry about right now.

"Sounds like working with him was a bad experience for you," I said.

"No, not really. But I did learn that pediatrics isn't my thing," Teresa replied. My attention wandered. I didn't want to hear any more about a boy who liked to run around the room after reading a few words in a book.

Because she went to college in Utah and stayed on to work there, Teresa had seen Sam only a few times—on her wedding day and during several brief overnight stops we made at her and Perry's apartment while traveling between California and Colorado.

Like all the other members of our extended family, she hadn't whispered a word of her concerns. Still, how could I expect her to be any different than anyone else, family or professional?

I read and read. Early autism researchers followed pretty poor paths of inquiry into its cause. People in the helping professions often inflicted even more pain on families and those with autism in their search for treatment. Sadly, we'd experienced much of that already. By the end of our holiday break, I had about all I could take of the books. However, upending one book after the other helped my mind make peace with my heart, which had felt the truth long before my head could bear it.

Favorite Books, Favorite Music

WE RETURNED TO THE NIMBUS GRAY SKIES of an upstate New York winter with our Christmas bounty, including several new toys for the boys and more winter clothes, something we didn't collect much of while living in California. Sam received three half-hour videotapes filled with Dr. Seuss books from Mark's aunt, a West Texas schoolteacher, for a Christmas present. He watched them on Mom and Dad's video player dozens of times before we left. With one book on each tape, the animators set Dr. Seuss's words in motion. Sam's eyes darted as capital *A* catapulted across the screen.

> *"BIG A*
> *little a*
> *What begins with A?"*

I hoped Sam might see the letter *a* and recognize the secret code of this squiggly shape: the first sound of "*Aunt Annie's alligator . . . . A . . a . . A.*" But at least something literary and artful held his attention for thirty minutes at a time.

We were finding places for the new stuff all around the living room floor, making the flat look like a kids' house where

"This makes me think of when Weebo took a picture of Flubber and it went crazy."

adults happened to live. As we unpacked the tapes, I remembered that Dr. Seuss had died a few months earlier, soon after the fall semester started. A cold front brought rain the day before. Since roads were nearly puddle-free by morning, I rode my bike to school. As I locked my bicycle into the rack beside the front steps of the music building, I noticed the *USA Today* headline announcing Theodor Geisel's death in the vending box nearby. I read most of the story without getting the paper out of the rack. My mind flashed to a foggy memory of Mom coaxing me, as a preschooler, through Dr. Seuss's *Hop on Pop*, teaching me how to read.

I inhaled some cold air to clear my head, walked up the steps into the building, and opened the classroom door. Now it was my turn to teach.

"Good morning!" I said. "Ready for more diminished seventh chords?"

Several students groaned as they pulled out blank sheets of manuscript paper and pencils. A few ceremoniously placed giant gum erasers next to their paper. My students had requested more music-dictation drills. Even though those drills wouldn't help their careers, I obliged them anyway, pounding out chords on the piano while they scrawled and scribbled melodies and harmonies, erased and scribbled some more.

"It has often been said there's so much to be read, you never can cram all those words in your head," Dr. Seuss's *I Can Read With My Eyes Shut!* cautioned Sam on the tape.

We were unpacking those tapes even though we had no way to play them in Rochester. Before moving to New York, we decided against packing the television, since it would take up too many cubic feet of space. Besides, we wanted to try living without one for a while.

"I think we should buy a little TV with a built-in video player," Mark said. "First of all, I'm tired of not having a TV."

His voice had an edge, as if he were expecting a fight.

"Besides, Sam follows the words and letters on those Dr. Seuss videos. We could get a small one with a built-in video player. It could help him learn to read."

He was ready for me to argue with him about whether we could afford it, but he knew the bank account balance as well as I did.

Would he tell me again how hard it was to be stuck inside during the winter? We had no backyard where Sam could run outdoors barefoot in just his training pants and T-shirt. The boys' Big Day Out was going to the coin-operated laundry and stopping afterward for candy at the drugstore. Sam ran around the busy laundry room, keeping track of the automatic cycles on all of the washers and dryers, not only the ones Mark was running, but also those of the other patrons.

"I never thought about getting a built-in," I said, refusing his challenge for a fight over the few discretionary dollars we had left. "That's a great idea. Plus, we can borrow other videos from the library."

We drove to the discount store and used our credit card to buy an off-brand television with a built-in video player. As Mark pulled the machine from the box, the box tipped over on the floor. Michael regarded it and crawled inside. I smiled.

"What is it with kids and boxes?" I asked.

"Did you know this unit comes with an adapter?" Mark said, ignoring my question. "We can plug it into the lighter in the car and the boys can watch videos when we travel."

Mark showed Sam how to insert the videotapes. Since doing that automatically turned on the television, too, Sam could watch without any help from Mark or me.

What is it with kids and gadgets? I wondered each time I watched Sam insert a video into the player.

I found myself observing Sam the way I imagined Maria Montessori watched her students. I watched Sam outgrow some of his fixations, such as turning toy cars upside down to spin the wheels. He still upended them occasionally, but other times he raced the little toy cars around the living room floor. He continued to fill reams of paper by painting his cubist rainbows, like an artist learning the vocabulary of his palette.

Our monthly trip to the public library provided Sam other chances to discover new worlds and learn new concepts. He never tired of Tana Hoban's picture books, which introduced him to abstract ideas. He woke up to tapes of cheery Raffi songs and fell asleep to artful lullabies. Sam's speech benefited from singing along. He sang along in the right key, too, Mark said. The best lullaby tape featured local star Jan DeGaetani singing Alec Wilder's night songs and lullabies. The tape was out of print, so I eventually made a bootleg copy. She sang so movingly, and in warm, clear tones. The first time Sam saw my tears as we listened, he got upset with me. I quickly blinked them back and tried to keep her tender voice from affecting me so deeply, at least not in front of him. Another night, I tried to sing one of the Wilder lullabies to the boys. Sam covered my mouth with his hands, his wild eyes begging me to stop.

Our weekly visits to the toy library, located in an old building on the edge of downtown, added even more to Sam's upward learning curve. The library staff piled the sturdy bookcases and tall metal shelves with hundreds of educational toys. I was thrilled to discover, tucked away on a top shelf, a collection of Montessori cylinders. Those cylinders had been too expensive to purchase and too complicated to make. Meticulously carved of maple and polished smooth, the varying cylinders gave Sam concrete experiences with abstract ideas like mass and volume. If he mismatched width or depth, the cylinders wouldn't fit in the corresponding hole. The materials, so appealing to the touch, inspired his patience. He never screamed at his mismatches. He simply tried again.

Sam found other toys he could sort or compare. He enjoyed measuring and pouring. He enjoyed playing and learning with almost every toy we borrowed from the toy library, except the mystery box. It was a shoe-sized box with a hand-sized hole in the side. Even if he watched me hide something inside it, he was afraid of reaching inside the smooth velvet lining to retrieve it himself. I didn't understand why, and neither did the toy librarian, after we explained why we brought the mystery box back early.

The librarian suggested Little Tikes toys for Sam. He pretended to do the laundry when we borrowed the kid-sized washer and dryer set. After he saw Michael climb inside and wheel from room to room in a miniature coupe, yelling "vroom, vroom," Sam was soon making "vroom" sounds all around the flat.

When we checked out a big, blue tumbling mat, both boys ran around in circles on top of the mat until Sam figured out how to Velcro the ends together, transforming it into a makeshift tube. He crawled inside and rolled the hollow log over and over, bumping from one side of the living room to the other. He figured out how to stand the whole thing up. He'd give Mark a cue for a gentle push and Mark obliged. Sam laughed and squealed "All fall down!" reciting a line from his favorite Helen Oxenbury book.

We were back in our Rochester routine. We didn't have to be embarrassed or afraid of teachers, therapists, or other outsiders judging us, making us insecure about any odd behavior of Sam's we decided to tolerate. No stranger's stares clouded our thinking about what was important.

But the television was inching us back. I wasn't sure I was ready to return to our busy California life. I wanted more time to observe, and think, and feel.

"And you don't have to stop. You can think about SCHLOPP. Schlopp. Schlopp. Beautiful schlopp. Beautiful schlopp with a cherry on top," the video told Sam. *"Oh, the THINKS you can think!"*

"You want wings for dinner?" Mark asked, bringing me back to the present moment.

"Sure," I said.

He pulled a package of chicken wings out of the refrigerator and rinsed them clean in the sink.

"Things are going to be so different when we get back home," he said, as if he had read my mind.

He dropped several naked wings into the oil-filled wok. Earlier that afternoon, he picked up two jars of wing sauce at Country Sweet. After the wings came out of the oil, I slathered them with the spicy sauce, wondering how to keep stocked after we moved back to California. I tried to replicate the recipe, but to no avail. Even Jan and Tracy knew of Country Sweet wing sauce and asked us to bring back jars for them.

The wings cooked up fast. I loaded the salad spinner with greens and set the spinner in front of Sam, who was sitting at his kid-sized kitchen table in the corner. Sam spun the bowl's handle as fast as he could, lifted the lid, and watched the greens flop down from the side as the spinning slowed. He laughed and spun, again and again, until the salad greens were bone dry.

I told Mark one thing that I was concerned for, back in California.

"I'm worried that I won't be able to look at Sam's baby pictures any more," I said.

I knew that came out of the blue. But the few photos we'd taken of the boys since moving to Rochester already looked different through this new prism. Before, I thought snapshots revealed the past. Now I recognized that my heart saw something of the future in them, too. Had Sam's future been stolen? I couldn't bear to look.

I expected the surprised look on Mark's face, but he didn't ask me for an explanation. He wanted to talk about what was bothering him the most.

"I'm really mad at the Sacramento schools," he said. "They should have figured out the autism thing from the beginning. They dropped the ball. Who knows how much time we've lost?"

"That's true. We needed them to help Sam so much more than they did," I said. "We still need a lot more information. They've told us very little that helps."

I rescued the dry greens from Sam and we sat down to the table to eat. I wondered whether the problem was more than just the Rules. Was there another reason why they didn't suggest autism?

Another memory returned, igniting my frustration. When we first visited Sam's preschool, I told one woman on Sam's special education team that he enjoyed playing Cosmic Osmo on the computer. I used my best educatorspeak to tell her that Sam picked up problem-solving skills from the game.

"Does the school have other simple computer games that could help him catch up?" I'd asked.

"Mrs. Wolfe, Sam needs to be with people and learn to interact with them, not with machines," she'd replied.

I had stared at her probably a half-minute too long, wondering how she ended up in such an influential position. She had an elegant suit and polished fingernails. Through her art-fully applied eye shadow and mascara, I saw her eyes were well rested. I also noticed that the long runs of her brunette curls were meant to look casual but were, in fact, perfectly in place. I decided that not only did she not have kids of her own, but she also had not taught kids of any kind—normal or special—in quite a while.

If I'd disregarded the Rules, she would have had to admit that she hardly knew Sam. But I didn't confront her.

Now, months later, her dismissive attitude toward me and my ideas made my face grow hot. Or maybe it was Country Sweet's spicy wing sauce.

"Are you all right, honey?" Mark asked.

"Yeah, I just remembered something about Sacramento," I said, stopping to drink some water.

I told him about that day. I was mad at myself the most.

"Why was I willing to bite holes in my tongue in order to make nice with her? Why didn't I stick up for Sam?" I asked.

"I know I wasn't there that day, but I know you," Mark said. "If she ticked you off, you probably said something that stuck it to her. Or you just stared at her in that way that you do. That stare cuts anyone down to size."

We laughed. Perhaps I needed my own Dr. Seuss videos playing in the background, maybe *The Lorax*, or *I Had Trouble in Getting to Solla Sollew*.

"*I learned there are troubles of more than one kind. Some come from ahead. And some come from behind. But I've bought a big bat. I'm all ready, you see. Now my troubles are going to have troubles with me,*" Dr. Seuss could coach me.

After dinner, I called Patti, Sam's nursery school teacher, to pick up the conversation that we began last fall.

Health Record

I sped through the niceties and got right to the point.

"Since we're pretty sure that Sam does have autism, I wonder what you think we ought to do next?" I asked Patti.

"My friend's son has autism," she said. "At one point, I remember that they went to the university hospital in Syracuse and saw someone there. And I read in the newspaper that the local autism group got a big grant to support families. Maybe you should call them, too."

I found the local autism society in the phone book and called. No one was there. The next day I called again. A volunteer answered. Her director was out of town at a conference, but would call me when she returned.

"Could you give me the number, please, of the university hospital in Syracuse?" I asked. "Someone suggested to us that it would be a good place to go."

The volunteer offered the name and number of a developmental pediatrician at the State University of New York Health Science Center in Syracuse. The words "developmental pediatrician" didn't sink in right away. We hung up before a question formed in my head: how does a developmental pediatrician differ from a plain pediatrician?

I called the hospital. The appointment secretary for Dr. James Copeland picked up the line. I took a deep breath and began telling Sam's story, the one I had told over and over again, to one educator or pediatrician after another. I was tired of telling The Sam Story. It felt like calling the phone company to request a repair, only to be passed from one department to another, telling the story again and again, wondering if I'd ever be able to talk to the person who could actually fix the line.

"I'm with Michael. That's it."

"So we suspect our son has autism, but we don't know for sure," I finished. "Is it possible to set up an appointment with Dr. Copeland?"

"Our first available appointment for an evaluation with Dr. Copeland is April 27," she said.

"That's so far off!" I protested.

It was, after all, the middle of January.

"I realize it seems a long time away. But we have to gather information on your son in the meantime. You'll need to have all his medical records sent to us. And we have a comprehensive parent information form that we send to you to fill out and get back to us."

Oh, no, not another one of those dig-out-the-baby-book parent-report forms, I thought. *This one will surely be the longest of all.*

I accepted the appointment time, exchanged addresses, and hung up.

After a moment, I remembered that one call to the Kaiser pediatric clinic would secure nearly all Sam's medical records except for one—his checkup when he was three.

We had switched his health insurance that year and I scheduled an appointment with the top pediatrician in town. Sam and I waited ninety minutes in all to see her. As she checked his measurements and listened to his heart and lungs, her manner became increasingly irritating to me. She was so cool and distant. How did she ever become so popular and respected? After the checkup, we drove over the H Street bridge up to a lab near Mercy General Hospital. We waited another hour at the lab to have Sam's blood drawn and to collect a urine sample. I drove back toward the bridge to fill Sam's vitamin prescription at a neighborhood pharmacy on H Street, thinking it would be quicker at that little shop than at the chain store in midtown.

I'd long since run out of things to keep Sam occupied so he wouldn't have a meltdown. At the pharmacy, our third stop, and Sam's third time out of the car seat, he unraveled. He cried so hard and for so long that the pharmacist gave us a sideways glance. At seven months pregnant, I was exhausted and nearly cried, too. The new insurance was not a step up for us, I decided, after that four-hour ordeal, and especially compared to an hour excursion around Kaiser's clinic departments to accomplish the same thing. I told Mark I wanted to switch back.

"It was really that bad?" Mark had asked.

"Yes, it really *was* that bad." I got tired of telling Mark that. "All little kids hate to wait, but you know Sam. He hates it *more*."

A few days later, a copy of the medical report recording that awful day arrived in our Rochester mailbox. As Mark rifled through the other mail, he handed the envelope to me. Another bad memory pushed forward as I read in the margin of Sam's growth chart, "Eye Contact?"

In an instant, I discovered that the whole overdrawn effort to get through a basic checkup had buried an opportunity to get to the core of Sam's problem. When the pediatrician had asked Sam a question, he didn't answer. "Sam's really not talking," I told her, explaining that I called the County Office of Education to arrange in-home speech therapy for Sam. I watched the pediatrician study Sam for a few seconds. Suddenly, her face changed as if another thought interrupted whatever she was preparing to say.

Another moment passed.

"You called the county? And they're coming out?" she asked. I nodded.

"Well, that should do," she said.

Her focus—barely on Sam and never quite on me—shifted somewhere toward the wall. That was when she wrote "Eye Contact?" on the chart that I was now, more than a year later, ruminating over. That was the last straw. The only help she offered was that prescription for vitamins. "He should have these," she said. "Those grocery vitamins have too much sugar in them."

Mark was busy studying the other mail.

"Mark," I said, shaking the copy of the medical record in front of him. "You've got to see this. Remember that awful day we had when he was three, with his checkup? Look at what the pediatrician wrote on the chart."

"You mean this here—'Eye Contact'?" he asked.

"Yes, that!"

I could feel my heart pounding in my ears.

"She wrote that on his growth chart without saying a word to me that she had a concern. How dare she say nothing! Why didn't she ask me if he made eye contact with us?"

"I'm sorry, honey, I don't get it," Mark said sheepishly. "Why is that such a big deal?"

"A big deal? I wish you would read even half the stuff I've read," I scolded him. "We've got a lot of work to do with Sam. Serious work. Lack of eye contact is one of the early indicators of autism. You need to know this stuff, too, and stop leaving it all to me. I mean, when exactly was this pediatrician planning on saying something to us? A year later? At his next checkup? She didn't ask me to bring him back in a few months. She didn't refer us to another physician. She didn't ask what the county had found, or what they were doing for him. Those two words were like a secret code to her. She must have learned something about the signs in medical school or somewhere. Those two words just say everything. She knew, and she said nothing, nothing at all to me. *Nothing*."

Mark's eyes fixed on me and fogged up. He did that when I was upset. It scared me. I wanted him to speak up. When I was little, I froze in fear whenever Dad got upset. But when Mark fought back, I felt less anxious. I didn't have to imagine what he might be thinking.

The local autism society's director returned my call. I told her that Sam had an appointment with Dr. Copeland in Syracuse.

"That's good," she said. "They're miles ahead in Syracuse. There's a lot going on there that could be helpful to you."

What might that mean? Patti had courage, calling to tell us what she thought might be wrong with Sam, far more courage than anyone in our family or in California. *People in Syracuse must be utterly fearless*, I thought.

"Well, the appointment is not until the end of April," I told her, resting my elbows on the kitchen windowsill and cradling the phone. Ice feathers glazed the window's edge. I took care not to lean against the glass for fear that it would stick to my skin. The colorless sky reflected the Genesee's hollow waters. Tree trunks and branches steeled against the cold, turning gray before my eyes.

"These are such dark days for us," I said. "We don't know what to do."

"Would you like me to come by for a visit?" she asked. "I'd like to meet Sam and we can talk."

"We'd like that very much," I said.

We arranged for a visit the following week.

That night, I would learn about Syracuse. The boys were asleep, giving me a chance to draft some of my research paper on the computer in our bedroom. Mark called me into the living room.

"Hey, you've got to see this. It's about autism, and it's in Syracuse," Mark said. A news anchor had announced the next story segment coming up on *20/20*, ABC's television news magazine.

I pushed back from the computer and rubbed my eyes as I walked into the living room. Mark wasn't sitting in the platform rocker. He was standing a few feet in front of the television set, his arms in front of his chest and holding his chin in his hands.

The program featured an education professor doing innovative, but controversial, work with children and young adults with autism. His clients couldn't speak at all. Some of them barely had control over their arms and legs, let alone the dozens of tiny facial muscles that must be harnessed in order to speak. But when adults sat next to them and helped them keep their typing hands steady, they typed whatever they had to say. They had smart, sophisticated ideas. Autism appeared to trap those ideas in their brains, an effect similar to cerebral palsy and other developmental disabilities that compromise muscle control.

"He's in there. Sam's in there," Mark said, his eyes so wet with tears that mine welled up, too, just looking at him. "We've got to get him out."

Mark was in the game.

At last.

Other Holidays

The local autism society director visited us at our flat, something she didn't normally do. She never told us why she made an exception for us. But whatever her reason, she opened a

"I used to blow the milk pod fairies off dandelions."

window into another world much larger than ours. She encouraged us to attend an upcoming autism conference in West Virginia, assuring us that we would gain an understanding of Sam's problems that had eluded us so far.

Exodus, I thought. *Maybe not to the Promised Land, but at least out of hell on earth.*

Mark studied the conference brochure and schedule, and began planning the entire trip—from where we would stay to how we would juggle the kids so that we could take turns attending sessions. The conference offered group child care, but they couldn't take Michael. Not quite one, he was too young for group care.

We drove through western Pennsylvania on a snowy weekend, but it was light and intermittent. New Yorkers called it lake-effect snow. Cold Canadian winds blew down over lakes Erie and Ontario and pulled up the moisture, freezing it and dropping it over the countryside.

Fastened snugly in their car seats, the boys were content looking out the windows at the frozen landscape. We crossed the bridge over the Kanawha River in the center of Charleston, West Virginia. I looked back over my shoulder across the river at the town which seemed old and wise, nestled among gnarled trees and steep hills that were older and wiser still.

We arrived in downtown Huntington just before suppertime. We checked into the conference hotel and settled in our room. I fed the boys some food that we'd packed and brought with us from Rochester. Mark rushed downstairs to hear Temple Grandin, the keynote speaker, over dinner. Grandin was an animal science professor at Colorado State University. By the time Mark came back, the boys had taken their baths and gone to sleep.

"Temple was amazing," Mark said. "She talked about her autism, but she also talked about what she does for a living. Do you know what she does? You'll never guess. She designs cattle chutes."

"What?" I asked. Why was I surprised by this? I didn't have any idea what a grown-up with autism might do, or not do, for a living. Teresa's belief that people with autism didn't live independently suddenly seemed outdated.

"Cattle chutes, you know, cattle-handling facilities and feedlots," Mark said with an excitement in his voice I hadn't heard in years, and certainly not about feedlots. "She lives fifteen minutes from your mom and dad! Anyway, you should see these facilities that she designs. They're, well . . . beautiful. She even designed one for John Wayne."

"Cattle-handling facilities," I echoed. "What does that have to do with autism?"

"Nothing, or maybe everything. You should have seen her talk about her work. She'd put up a slide and say, 'Isn't that beautiful?' and it really was. You'll have to hear her talk sometime. She talked about autism, too, of course. One of the boys on the *20/20* program was there. Once in a while he would groan or make some other noise. Eventually, Temple couldn't tune it out any more. The groans got her off track. You could tell autism mannerisms would distract her, even though they didn't bother anyone else. That was interesting. After a while, she said that if he couldn't stop groaning, he'd have to leave. So he left. At first I wasn't sure what to think about that. It didn't seem fair, but everyone else in the room seemed okay with it."

Temple had written a book about her childhood. Mark wanted to read it right away. But it was past ten o'clock and we were all tired from the trip. We went to bed.

The next morning, after we both read the description of Margaret Bauman, a brain researcher from Harvard University, Mark decided to take the boys out to explore Huntington.

"You've got a much better chance of understanding what she's going to say than I do," he said.

I wasn't so sure, but it was my turn to hear a session. As I entered the hotel ballroom, I could tell that it was filled with plenty of parents and other non-medical types. Dr. Bauman stepped up to the speaker's podium. She asked her assistant to dim the lights and turn on the slide projector.

Dr. Bauman told us how each one of the six boys with autism was selected for her study.

"You might think that we would have at least one girl among the subjects, but we don't. Perhaps that's because most people with autism are males," Dr. Bauman said. "You also might notice that we have two subsets among our six subjects. Three boys came to us around age twelve; the other three boys came to us in their early twenties."

She never identified them by name, but she clearly felt a close connection to her research subjects even though they were dead. She explained how each boy died and how their donation of brain tissue came to her.

Suddenly, I got scared. As children with autism grew, did new risks emerge?

One boy had drowned.

"He was an expert swimmer and was on his school's swim team. No one's quite sure what happened," she said.

Some inexplicably suffered strokes.

Another boy died of appendicitis.

"He obviously had been in pain for some time, but wasn't able to tell anyone until he was moribund," Dr. Bauman said.

My eyes shifted away from the podium to the handout. I doodled in the margins, trying to regain my focus. Sam was a yeller, but when he was sick, he got quiet. How were we going to figure this stuff out? When was someone going to sit down and tell us all the risks and how we were supposed to deal with them? Did anyone know?

My attention returned to Dr. Bauman just as she began talking about her set of control variables: a slide bank of normal brain tissue created by Nazi doctors researching the brain under the Third Reich.

"It's hard to think that anything good could come from such inhumanity, but we can choose to make it so," she said.

She told us how she and her research assistants prepared the boys' brain tissue for the slides and made the side-by-side comparisons from the German databank, using grids to count the cells.

"Essentially, we look into our microscopes and count the cells in each grid with click-counters," she said. "So, you see, medical research isn't as glamorous as you might think."

Light laughter bounced around the room. I imagined Dr. Bauman and her research assistants. Peer into the eyepiece, upper left. Click. Click, click, click. Click, click. Boring. But Sam wouldn't think it was boring. He'd enjoy it. After he was done clicking and counting for the day, he would click his clicker as fast as he could, watching the numbers go by for fun.

She told us which parts of the autistic brains were different from the Nazi-prepared brain tissue. Not damaged, she was careful to say, but different.

"We found that two parts of the brain differ. All the rest of brain is the same. In these two parts of the brain, there are many more cells. They are smaller and much more tightly packed than the others. As you look further at each individual cell, you will see that they have fewer synapses, or connections to one another, than among normal cells."

To illustrate, she likened cell synapses to an elaborate rosebush in the normal brain. A normal brain had many routes for one cell to transmit information to another cell. But in those two areas of the autistic brain, there were fewer routes to transmit the information. However, those routes looked more deeply carved.

"As we were making this discovery, I went back into our clinic to be around the kids, and I looked at their autistic behavior in a new way," she said. "Perhaps their repetitive behaviors were a deliberate attempt to make those needed connections in their brains."

She explained the behaviors associated with the parts of the brain. One part was responsible for social interaction, especially the reptilian fight-or-flight response. Another part was responsible for processing the five senses. She also told us that doctors currently had no diagnostic tool to see whether a patient's brain cells were growing this way. This tightly packed brain cell growth could only be seen forensically.

During the question-and-answer session, audience members asked many questions that I wanted to ask. One asked Dr. Bauman what she suspected might cause autism, based on her research.

"I have my own ideas, of course," she replied. "Because the affected parts of the brain develop very early, at about ten to twelve weeks gestation, and because it happens more often in first-borns than in successive births, it's possible that hormone imbalances play a part."

I couldn't wait to tell Mark about all I learned. We met for lunch.

"First of all," I told him, trying not to talk with food in my mouth, "you would have understood what she was saying. She knew she was talking to a roomful of regular people, and parents of people with autism, especially. She explained everything in plain English."

I drew pictures of brains and normal and autistic cells for him on a piece of scrap paper. Based on what Dr. Bauman said, I suggested to Mark that some of Sam's repetitive behaviors and fixations might be helpful instead of harmful.

"I don't think we should call them *stims* anymore," I said. We picked up that term from the special education people in Sacramento. It was shorthand for yet another piece of jargon, *self-stimulating behavior*. I knew that meant the behavior simply needed more observation and understanding. But I'd heard teachers and therapists apply the term to any kind of behavior that they found annoying, too. If we took our time observing and studying it, I told Mark, we might discover how to help Sam. Or we might decide to leave some things alone, since some behaviors might accomplish their purpose and he would outgrow them.

"Maybe he will be able to do more for himself than we believe," I said.

"We'll still have to see that doctor in April, because at least someone can tell us for sure," Mark said.

Did Mark think I doubted our need to do that? Sure, we were on the right path. But I wanted reinforcement, too, like those road signs marking "U.S. 50" and "East" that confirmed we were on our way.

"Dr. Bauman also thinks the disorder may be hormone-related," I said. "It wasn't part of her study, but she said that the two parts of the brain that were affected by autism develop at ten to twelve weeks."

"That's when you almost miscarried."

Mark connected the same dots that I did.

"Did that cause it?"

"I have no idea," I said, yet I felt I was lying, because I had thought about that plenty since leaving the hotel ballroom.

"It could be a sort of chicken-and-egg thing. Did I start to miscarry because something was going wrong in Sam's brain development, and then stopped because something made itself right again? Or did the bleeding affect his brain development? I don't know. We'll probably never know."

I didn't tell him about my darkest thoughts, the ones about my eating disorder, how my periods had stopped, and in the middle of my recovery I started taking the Pill in college but I couldn't tolerate it, so I'd stopped taking it. What would Mark think if I said that out loud?

Mark wanted to attend a lecture about sensory integration and other educational interventions, so I stayed with the boys for the afternoon. I tried to read some of Dr. Bauman's handouts, including her most recent research paper, but I had trouble deciphering all the medical terms. She seemed to be addressing a different audience with her paper than the one she addressed at the conference. Reading the paper made me sleepy, so I took an afternoon nap with the boys.

At dinner, I was glad I had taken a nap. Mark was excited about all he had learned and I could barely keep up with all he shared.

"You know, we're hearing from the best in the business at this conference," he said. "We'll want to remember a lot of these names in the future. So far, the best speakers were the professors from Division TEACCH in North Carolina, and an expert, Lorna King, in a kind of occupational therapy called sensory integration. She talked about a lot of things that we're doing with Sam already. Her ways of handling autistic kids helps them stay calm so they can learn."

"What do you mean?"

Could we be doing something right for a change?

"Rolling him up inside a tumbling mat, for one. And all those bike rides on the canal trail, bouncing him around in the bike carrier," he said.

"What? How?" Mark wasn't making any sense.

"Kids with autism can't handle all the input coming from their senses," Mark said. "It's like everything is coming in on high. Bouncing around helps them calm down and get their brain organized. Actually, I can kind of relate to that."

Mark's comments initially didn't make much sense, but I started to connect the ideas. How many times had a bike ride invigorated me and helped me think more clearly? The concept matched up with what Dr. Bauman said about the parts of the brain that were different. Sam couldn't sit and listen to his teacher read a book in circle time because he couldn't predict if, or when, a classmate might bump or touch him.

That night, as the boys bathed in the hotel tub together, I recalled that, when Sam was Michael's age, we brought him in the shower with us. He wiggled too much in the bath and slipped from our grip, sliding under the water so many times that we decided the tub was no place for Sam. Other babies will instinctively gasp for air as the water rains down on them from a shower head, but not Sam. He found the pulsating spray soothing.

Sam hardly ever let us hug or kiss him. Now we realized he probably never would.

My spring classes moved at a more furious pace than they had in the fall. A fellow student suggested that I take the French equivalency exam, since I had a year of it in high school. Even though by taking the exam I would earn another master's degree and move me closer to my goal of earning a doctorate, I couldn't muster the enthusiasm for it.

Another student had taken me aside to clue me in on what it was going to take to finish. "You should know that some of us figured this out and it takes an average of nine years to get a Ph.D. here," Alan said.

"How can anyone afford nine years of school here?" I asked. Tuition was sky high and the school offered few scholarships for students like me.

"I don't like to think about how much I owe," he replied. Alan had been there a long time. I knew him when I finished my performance degree six years ago. He was working on his master's degree, too.

"I requested that this year qualify for my residency, and they granted that. I've got it in writing," I protested.

"Look at the class schedule," Alan said. "All the professors take the summer off. There are never any advanced theory classes in the summer. I don't know why no one cautioned you about it, but someone should have told you that up front. It won't matter that you completed your residency. You'll have to be here at least one more academic year to finish."

For my music career to have any longevity, I needed a college job. I played professionally after graduating, but I couldn't make enough money at it. Even as I was working part-time for the arts council, I asked about work at the smaller colleges and junior colleges in Sacramento. The music dean at Cal State, Sacramento, told me that they needed performers who could also teach some academic classes. I liked music theory—exploring the structure and form of music—but learning more was essential for me to teach at the college level. Yet after what Alan shared, my hopes were melting. We couldn't afford another year in Rochester.

We came to Rochester to rescue our careers and rescued our son instead. As we planned our return to California, Mark knew he could at least step back into his old orchestra job, as tenuous as the symphony's finances would be that fall. No matter what happened, Mark would still be able to work—he had greatly expanded his repertoire and his network in the past year. But I remained adrift, with no clear direction in sight. I had some inkling where Sam was going to go, but I didn't know what I was going to do.

Footprints

Spring break came and went, and before we knew it, it was April 27, Sam's appointment day with Dr. Copeland. The hospital staff told us to bring only Sam. Patti agreed to watch Michael for the day.

Syracuse was a two-hour drive from Rochester. Since Sam's appointment was at nine o'clock, we were at Patti's house a little after seven. Patti had moved her nursery school to the two front rooms of her home after church officials decided to start their own program, so Michael would spend the morning with the "big kids" in nursery school.

In return for the favor of watching Michael, we brought Patti our little fish tank shaped like a giant crayon. We hoped the children in Patti's nursery school would enjoy the tank as much as Sam did. We bought the tank and a blue betta fish to brighten the long winters, and to teach Sam something about caring for, and appreciating, living things. "Just a small pinch, Sam," we would say when he dropped in the little flakes of fish food. He giggled as he watched the fish attack its dinner until it was devoured. Sam pushed up a chair so he could watch the

"I might get bothered pretty easily."

fish swim in a plastic bowl while Mark or I cleaned the tank each week.

It was cloudy and cold as we drove east on Interstate 95 toward Syracuse. On the radio, the weatherman called for sunny skies later in the day. Mark was tired of the long, upstate winter. Bright white snowdrops came up first, and now they were yielding to colorful crocuses. That was spring to me. But until all the snow was melted, Mark said it was still winter.

We arrived in Syracuse about fifteen minutes early. We found the hospital and followed the attendant's directions to our spot in the parking lot. We checked in with the receptionist in pediatrics and took a seat as she announced our arrival. I didn't try to prepare Sam for what to expect in the doctor's office because I didn't know what to expect either. I hoped it wouldn't be a repeat of that horrible day the city school personnel evaluated Sam.

Dr. Copeland greeted Mark and me with a warm handshake. He extended his hand to Sam. Sam looked at his hand, and regarded Dr. Copeland for a minute. Dr. Copeland wore sturdy, horn-rimmed glasses and kept his salt-and-pepper beard impeccably groomed. I'm sure Sam would have liked to touch the doctor's beard if he could.

Dr. Copeland took us to the exam room, and as he waved his arms about, he explained that this was a teaching hospital and a number of students would watch the exam in an adjoining room. We passed the viewing room on the way into the examination room. I felt a wave of heat radiating from the students packed inside. Several students looked our way as we passed by. Others tried to look away, as if mutual privacy were assured so long as we didn't acknowledge each other's existence.

The examination room looked like a cross between a pre-school room and a conference room. There were no windows, just the two-way mirror between us and the students. The clean, gray-and-brown carpet was woven from dark, heavy wool, which made me itch to look at it. Dr. Copeland extended his hand to Sam again, this time handing over a couple of worn, wooden blocks.

His eyes focused on Mark and me. He started his line of questioning.

"When did Sam start walking by himself?"

"When did Sam start crawling?

"How many months did he crawl? And how many months did he walk with your help?"

Same old, same old. Two or three more of these unimaginative questions and I've got a diagnosis for you, I thought.

But before my frustrations burst out of my mouth—"Did you even read that parent report you asked for in advance?"—something stopped me. I sensed a method in his line of questioning. I just couldn't figure out what it was.

"Can he walk the stairs one at a time? Up the stairs? How about down?"

I never thought about that. No one had ever asked.

"Can he ride a tricycle?"

Dr. Copeland kept asking about important milestones in Sam's growth and development that no one had asked about before. I wondered if Mark was noticing it, too. Dr. Copeland's questions kept us talking about Sam, but connecting the dots in new ways.

We weren't just filling in the blanks in Sam's baby book any more. We were telling Sam's story, the whole story. Mark and I were so engrossed that Dr. Copeland's pivotal question—

"When did you first think something was wrong?"—came and went. We both answered it matter-of-factly.

I noticed that Sam wasn't able to reach the light switch in the room. He was busy banging the blocks together. Dr. Copeland asked for the blocks back. Sam obliged and Dr. Copeland handed him a little wooden truck next. Sam turned it upside down and spun the wheels for a moment before rolling it back and forth on a table top. Dr. Copeland began asking Sam a series of questions. Sam pointed to his nose, but he had to be asked twice. Dr. Copeland also tried to prompt several kinds of play that Sam had never done and wouldn't do after he was asked. After Dr. Copeland was sure that Sam had heard him, he pressed no further. Sam went back to play with the little wooden truck.

"Well, we're done here," Dr. Copeland said. I was surprised. I thought this would take all day. It felt like we'd just started. I tipped my head, glancing across the table at Dr. Copeland's watch. I calculated that we had been in the exam room about two hours. I admired Dr. Copeland's calm demeanor and efficiency. His questions bore deeply into problems in a way that we'd not considered before. Gathering up my memories that compared and contrasted—from Dr. Copeland's evaluation of Sam to Nancy's and the school's—I had the urge to tell the students how fortunate they were to witness top-notch work.

"Why don't you get some lunch and be back by one o'clock," Dr. Copeland told us. "I'll come back to talk with you after that. I'll be conferring with the students in the meantime."

We left the examination room, walking past the students lurking behind the mirror. Their door was now open, perhaps to improve air circulation. They all looked our way as we walked by. Their gazes were different than we went in.

What was that look? I wondered. *The price of witnessing . . . a loss of innocence?* I noticed that Mark didn't look their way as we passed by and wondered why. My stomach grumbled. Breakfast seemed so long ago. I figured Sam and Mark must be as hungry as I was. I stopped wondering about the students' collective gaze.

We returned a few minutes before one o'clock and were escorted to a different room. This one looked more like a typical examining room, except it had a long window along one wall. Dr. Copeland spent a minute or two checking Sam over physically, listening to his heart and lungs, and checking his reflexes. Dr. Copeland sat down in a chair by the window and introduced the three people who had joined us in the room. Two were social workers, and the third, a liaison with the university's preschool. The three women began to line up behind Dr. Copeland's chair as he sat in front of the window. One of the social workers thought better of it and moved closer to where Mark and I were sitting.

Sam found the light switch. But flipping it back and forth had little effect. The sun was perched high in the sky, dispatching the clouds and sending in warm, bright rays of light.

"It as you suspected. Sam has autism," Dr. Copeland began.

I heard Mark draw a sharp breath. Or maybe it was me.

The room suddenly filled with silhouettes.

I couldn't feel the floor anymore, but I wasn't falling. I was floating without water. No ceiling or walls. No chair. My shoulders tried to center my heart. I heard another sharp breath. That one was definitely mine.

Tears swelled in my eyes. I blinked, but they escaped and began rolling down my cheeks. One of the silhouettes handed me a tissue.

I heard a third sharp breath.

It was Dr. Copeland's.

"I'm sorry," he said. "I thought you all knew this. I'm sorry."

My feet searched for the floor.

Had we put on that good of a show? He probably had a different talk planned for parents who weren't ready, I thought.

"Honestly, Dr. Copeland, I thought so, too," I said. "I'm sorry. I don't know why I'm crying all of a sudden."

"It's because when you say it, it makes it real," Mark said. I looked at him, a puddle of tears, too.

Sam continued to flip the light switch. The silhouettes slowly became people again.

"Actually it's a relief," I said. "We don't have to wonder any more."

I blew my nose into the tissue. Mark put his arms around me. I rested my head on his shoulder for a second or two, and then sat up straight. We held hands across each other's laps waiting for Dr. Copeland to speak. When he did, I sensed a change in the way he chose his words and the tone of his voice. He spoke more slowly.

Were those phrases ones he might use for parents who weren't ready to hear "Your child has autism"?

He identified things in Sam's current behavior, and the way Sam had grown up, that, when taken together, led to his conclusion. He reminded us that there was no test he could perform to corroborate an autism diagnosis. But he felt that Sam, at four years and five months old, had all the telltale signs.

"However, I would like to recommend that your son's regular pediatrician order a test for Fragile X," Dr. Copeland said. "I can do that in my written report."

I remembered hearing a little about Fragile X Syndrome at the conference in West Virginia. This sub-type of autism had a genetic origin. I understood why Dr. Copeland was recommending the test. If we were carriers, there was a risk to our future children. A fear for Michael's well-being momentarily raced through my head. But my heartbeat stayed steady. Something about the both of the boys' strong physicality told me that Fragile X was not part of their stories, so I didn't press Dr. Copeland for more information.

"It will take me a few weeks to write up the results in my report," Dr. Copeland said. "I will address it to Sam's regular pediatrician and I'll send you a copy."

He paused and gave us his prognosis.

"I'm confident that when Sam is fourteen or fifteen years old, his autism won't be readily apparent to most people."

Wouldn't be readily apparent? Looking at Sam, still flipping the light switch, I felt my eyebrows pop up for a second. That was hard to believe.

"All kids with autism are a little different from one another," he said. "But I think you'll see how well he will adapt."

Dr. Copeland knew we were going back to California. But he wanted us to understand what the best practices in teaching and therapy looked like, so we would know what to ask for after we returned home. He said that was his reason for inviting the social workers and the preschool's liaison.

"In fact, if you have some time this afternoon, I recommend that you visit the preschool and see what they are doing."

The social workers handed us their cards, and the liaison directed us to the school.

The teachers and children were winding up their day when we arrived. The integrated classroom looked so different from the program back in Sacramento. The liaison explained that it was important for kids with autism to learn and play in the company of "normal" children. Children with autism could master the same academic lessons and learn social skills better that way, she said.

She explained that their teachers adapted the classroom to meet all the children's needs. The teachers observed each child and developed a program that suited their individual needs.

I tried to pick out the kids with autism or other learning disabilities. It wasn't easy. The room hummed with activity. I had to focus on each student for a long time. I managed to pick out one or two children and that was only because they had longer interactions with their teachers.

I thanked the liaison, wondering whether anything like their program existed in California. As if she read my mind, she recommended that we buy one of the school's teaching manuals that outlined the best practices for integrated classrooms. I asked for contact information to order the book.

It was almost four o'clock by the time we left the hospital. We soaked in the late afternoon sunlight as we walked across the parking lot to our car. I noticed that Mark held his chest up high as he walked. While I was visiting with the liaison, Mark and Sam roamed around the school, tried out the playground, and left with a warm impression of the place, too.

"Sam really liked that school," Mark said, as we headed back to the interstate. "I wish there was something like this in California. Syracuse has it all over everybody."

"Maybe we should try to get him into one of the Montessori schools," I said. "Since the orchestra still works evenings, I can get a day job that pays well enough that we can afford the tuition and not go in too deep for child care."

"Do you think anyone would take him?" Mark asked.

After watching the 20/20 program, attending the conference, and visiting with Dr. Copeland, I realized Sam understood a lot more than we thought he did. In fact, I was beginning to think Sam understood everything we were saying. I glanced at the back seat. Thank goodness Sam was sleeping.

"You know, I think we should be more careful from now on what we say around Sam," I said.

"You're right, you're right. I'm sorry," he said.

"It's okay. He's asleep right now," I said, noticing that Mark was peeking in the rearview mirror to see for himself. "Sam did fine with Patti and the nursery school this year. There's no reason to think he wouldn't do fine in a Montessori school, especially with how he responded to the Syracuse school. I think a Montessori school would better fit his learning style than what the school district offers."

"I hadn't thought about it that way," Mark said. "But don't give people more credit than you should. Sacramento is far behind compared to here."

I was happy to get back to Patti's. Michael was still nursing a few times a day. Although he was accustomed to waiting, I was relieved. Even though Michael was thirteen months old, I hadn't thought much about weaning him. Sam weaned himself, earlier than I planned—earlier than the surgeon general was recommending at the time. Nursing until age two was not only acceptable, but preferable for health reasons. I felt a little self-conscious nursing Michael in front of Patti, but it left quickly.

I can think about this weaning stuff later.

Mark was excited to share our insights on autism with Patti. And I could see that she was happy that she had set us on the right path. She was curious about Dr. Copeland's prediction that by the time Sam turned fourteen or fifteen years old, most people would see Sam as any other normal teenager.

"I'm sorry I won't see that," she said. "You guys will send pictures once in a while?"

"Absolutely," Mark said.

There was a long silence.

"You must really enjoy this big hill behind your house in the winter," Mark said. "Can you sled on it?"

Mark and the boys went sledding a lot. We bought a couple of inexpensive flying saucers at the discount store. They learned to enjoy the cold, except when bits of snow got wedged between their mittens and their wrists.

"Not too much," Patti replied. "But maybe you know that on the other side of that hill is where all the lilacs are. In the spring, when they have the lilac festival, it just smells wonderful. You can smell them here, from clear on the other side of the hill."

"What is this? Tell me more," I asked, vaguely remembering something about Rochester and lilacs.

"You guys should go to the festival," Patti said. "You'll still be here when all the lilac bushes are in bloom. There are so many varieties. You wouldn't believe all the different colors and sizes. People come out just to stroll among the bushes. When the lilacs bloom, you know that spring is finally here."

We thanked Patti for watching Michael and for recommending the university hospital in Syracuse.

With just one more week of nursery school for Sam, we wanted to help him make a memory book so he could remember his nursery school friends after we returned to California. Patti agreed to help prepare the book.

As I wrapped up my own schooling, I talked to my major professor about finishing my master's project over the summer. He didn't think that I could make it by summer's end. Although I had never missed that kind of deadline before, I took his advice and picked up the paperwork to request an incomplete in case I needed it.

By design, my entire year's coursework led up to the writing of my final project. I wanted to finish. Yet I knew if I surrendered this dream, all my dreams might come true.

Our Baby's Homecoming

We started packing up the flat, giving away things like the sled saucers and snowsuits that we had no use for in sunny Sacramento. Mark sold the Subaru and bargained with several dealerships by phone for a minivan. He found one at a Virginia dealer near his mom's Alexandria townhouse, a Chrysler minivan spacious enough and reliable enough to get us and our belongings back to California.

We stopped packing one afternoon to attend the lilac festival. Patti was right about all the varieties. There were white and pink and fuchsia and magenta and light blue and dark blue and purple. The sweet, heady fragrance of lilacs wafted everywhere and helped us forget about the pressure and anxiety of moving again.

Sam stopped and squatted, pointing at a dandelion gone to seed.

"What's that?" he asked.

"Milk pod fairies," I said, remembering a part of the *Fantasia* movie that he and Michael watched over and over.

"Watch this!" Mark said. He squatted down, plucked up the dandelion, blew off the seeds and discarded the stem.

"Milk pod fairies!" Sam shouted, clapping his hands stiffly.

From his stroller, Michael watched the seeds float away, giggling.

Sam picked up another dandelion and blew off the fairies himself. He found another and another. We forgot all about the lilacs.

"Now that's funny. I used to push a stroller behind Grandpa.
I'm taking a risk. Ronnie wondered if it was fun."

Even with all the extra space afforded by the minivan, we had a hard time fitting everything we needed to pack on moving day. I could not remember where all the new stuff came from. The television and my bicycle were the only big things that we bought in Rochester. We'd given away so many things, too. We went to a bike shop to buy a rooftop rack for both my bike and the tandem. It was nearly dark when Mark finished assembling the rack and we finally pulled away. We drove about two hours to Jamestown when it started to snow. We were too tired to go any further and had to get a room in an old, two-story hotel.

"We couldn't even get one state behind us," Mark said, exasperated. "Does winter ever end here?"

I didn't know what to say. We didn't have to hurry back. We had leased our house through August to a young architect. He and his wife just had a baby boy. They were taking good care of the house and even planted a garden. Neither of us had the heart to ask them to leave early. Instead, we planned to spend the rest of the summer in Windsor with Mom and Dad. They were back for good from Saudi Arabia.

Windsor hadn't changed much since Mom and Dad moved there the day after I graduated from New London Senior High School. With beautiful Rocky Mountain vistas and dry desert air, a summer in Windsor was almost the same as a summer in a quaint resort. Mom, Dad, and my sisters would look after the boys so that Mark and I could finally have some time alone. I was looking forward to the help.

Traveling all day, we made it as far as La Salle, Illinois. It felt like we bypassed spring altogether and went straight to summer in one day. Mark's mood brightened. We stopped for dinner and found a Holiday Inn in the middle of nowhere. We were surprised to learn they had only one room available. It had an oversized tub with a waterfall faucet and spa jets in it.

Did we mind? the clerk asked. For just twenty dollars more than the basic rate, we said okay. Splashing around in a big tub sounded like a fun way to spend the evening.

The boys jumped in and began paddling around, playing with the water jets before the tub was even half full. Sam dipped his hands in the stream of water coming from the faucet, giggling. He looked up as Mark came in.

Mark wasn't laughing. He was fuming. I asked him why he was upset.

"You know we can't leave our instruments in the vehicles," he said. "You could help me bring in the suitcases and stuff, too."

"I brought in what I could, Mark. I couldn't leave the boys alone in the tub."

"You could have made them wait."

"But they're so tired from being buckled up all day. What else was I going to do? Chase after them all over the parking lot *and* unload?"

I sat in a stupor, looking at Mark.

The boys and I weren't depending on Mark to sacrifice himself for us, but I doubted that he believed it.

His anger spilled over easily the past few weeks, despite the progress we'd made with Sam—or perhaps because it was finally underway.

Mark knew of grief's isolation. His father left home when he was four years old. I never knew Homer. He died before Mark and I were married. Mark had watched and waited as I waded through my fear and bargaining over Sam's autism. Now it was my turn to wait. Like one of those chain-reaction car wrecks in the tule fog, we'd been blinded, slamming into one another as we tried to make our way around the carnage.

At the end of our third day on the road, we arrived in Windsor. Nineteenth-century farmers made modest fortunes growing sugar beets in the area and the town sprang to life at the foot of their sugar mill. Sturdy, well-kept houses lined streets named after trees such as Elm, Walnut, and Oak, if they ran east to west—or numbers, if they ran north to south. The sugar mill slumbered on 0 Street for decades before Mom and Dad ever moved into their house at Tenth and Locust.

We pulled up in front of Mom and Dad's sprawling ranch-style home of rock and cedar. We must have been a sight: a pickup truck with California license plates pulling a rented trailer with New York plates and a minivan with Virginia tags boasting a rooftop bike rack with a tandem attached.

As we unbuckled the boys, Mom and Dad rushed out the door to greet us. My sister Karen was right behind them. She must have come up from Denver. Dad told Mark to back the trailer onto the driveway. I was prepared to help unpack and unload this time. I knew the boys would be fine inside the house or the back yard on their own. A few minutes later, Chris and Ronnie arrived. Mom must have called them at their place a few blocks away to come and lend a hand.

We aren't by ourselves any more. We have lots of help, I thought.

Mom carried some of the toys from the van into the house. Mark and I grabbed suitcases. As we went up and down the stairs, she began telling me about her plans for the summer. In the mornings, we could walk to the new coffee shop a friend had just opened. In the evening, we could take walks by following the new jogging path that circled the lake. She thought the boys would enjoy the little footbridge on the north side, where an irrigation ditch channeled the lake's water out to the cornfields. She mentioned her friend, Kitty, who had just graduated with a master's degree in speech pathology and wanted to work with Sam.

"Would that be all right?" Mom asked.

"Of course," I said.

This could be the best help Sam has had since those few short months Nancy worked with him, I thought. *Had it been more than a year?*

"I didn't get to the grocery store, though," Mom said. "We'll have to go to Stefan's Market and get some things."

"That's fine," I said, and started to unpack a few days' worth of clothes for the boys. "Mark said he needed a few things from the store, too, so we can all go in the minivan as soon as he gets the trailer unhooked."

Our rooms filled up fast with boxes, suitcases, and toys. My computer went in the sun room along with Mark's tubas. There, among the plants and wicker furniture, I would finish my master's project and Mark would practice. Mark and I would sleep in the basement bedroom, and the boys would share the big family room beside it. It was cool and quiet and dark downstairs. I looked forward to many good nights of sleep.

"Are you ready to go to the store?" Mark shouted from the dining room.

"Just a second," I shouted back. Mom and I moved in a few more boxes and suitcases. Several minutes later we caught up with Mark upstairs.

"Let's get the boys and go."

Michael was playing with a toy car in the living room.

"Where's Sam?" Mark asked.

"Did you look in the backyard?" I replied.

"I'll check," Mom answered.

Mark swept up Michael and handed him to me.

"Check if he's still in the basement," I told Mark.

I tried to remember where I last saw Sam. Was he out front looking at the timer for the sprinklers? I walked toward the front door with Michael on my hip and Dad came inside.

"Was Sam out front with you?" I asked him.

"No, he wasn't," Dad said, setting the last box down on the living room floor.

Mom came from the back of the house.

"He's not in the backyard," she said.

Mark came up the basement stairs two by two.

"He's not in the basement. He's not in the house at all."

"My god, where is he?" I gasped. With that, Mom, Dad, Chris, Karen, and Ronnie scattered outside. Everyone was yelling his name.

"Sam?"

"Sam!"

I put Michael back down on the living room floor, thinking Sam might have walked over to the side yard of the house to look through the fence at the neighbor's dog. He wasn't there.

Mark grabbed the van keys. I followed him toward the van. As he began to back out of the driveway, I yelled, "Where are you going?"

"To the store," he shouted back, as he slipped into first gear and floored it.

I stood frozen.

Sam had been to Stefan's Market several times before, but would he really walk by himself?

It was about five blocks away, not much more of a walk, really, than the old walk around the block back in Sacramento. But I remembered Walnut Street and my heart began to pound. Walnut Street was busy. Locals used Walnut Street to get from one side of town to the other without having to bother with the trucks, traffic, and stoplights on Main Street. Sam couldn't get to the market without crossing Walnut Street. Stefan's was on the far side of the parking lot.

Would Sam even cross at the crosswalk and walk along the other shops in the strip mall, or would he cut across the lot among all those parked cars?

I couldn't imagine what Mark would find. I didn't want to know.

Mom and I were near panic. Dad, who usually got annoyed when he thought we were overreacting, was shaking. The crisis eased when we saw the van coming back down Tenth Street about five minutes later. I saw two shadows in the front, a big one on the driver's side and a little one on the passenger's side.

"I see him," Mom said. "He's got him. He's got Sam."

Dad returned to being annoyed, but waited in the driveway to hear Mark's story.

"Where was he?" I asked, as Mark got out of the van.

Sam unbuckled himself, got out, slammed the van door, and ran past Mom and Dad into the house.

"He was at the store," Mark answered. "He was going in and out of the automatic doors."

"Had anyone noticed? Was anyone trying to talk to him?" I asked.

"A few of the clerks were looking at him as if he was being kind of strange. Maybe they thought we were still in the parking lot and he had run ahead. I don't know. If much more time had gone by, they would have been checking things out more, I'm sure," he said.

I tried to imagine how that scene might have played out. A kindly clerk might have tried to talk to Sam, and he would have ignored her. The clerk might have gone to the manager, pointing at Sam while he stomped on the mats, running in and out the automatic doors. The manager might have made an announcement over the loudspeaker.

"Would the parents of a lost boy please come to the front of the store?"

That likely would have gotten Sam's attention. Then what would he have done? Would he have started to run around the store looking for us? Maybe a customer who was uncomfortable with Sam's odd behavior might have stormed up to the store manager to tell her how awful Sam's behavior was, just how bad were young parents these days, and when are you going to do the right thing and call the police?

Enough.

My head hurt from thinking about it. Anticipating how the rest of the world might interact with, or react to, Sam drained much of my energy these past four years. Sometimes I could anticipate and prevent Sam from being a nuisance or doing things that irked people. But most of the time, I failed, having no more to show for my effort than sweat down my back and under my breasts.

I'm not going to be embarrassed of Sam anymore. He can just be who he is. If he ever makes an actual mistake, we'll just fix it, I decided.

"I'm glad you thought of going to the store," I told Mark. "What made you think of it?"

"With everyone going in and out and everywhere, I figured Sam might have thought that we left without him."

"Why on earth would he think that?" I asked, mostly to myself.

Mark didn't answer me. He went back into the house to gather Michael and Sam so we could go to the market.

I started thinking about Mark's theory. Maybe he was right. Maybe Sam sorted out those cues from our chaotic arrival scene that made sense to him and reacted as best he could. Maybe Sam heard "store" and, remembering the automatic doors, decided he couldn't wait for us in order to test his latest cause-and-effect hypothesis: step on the mat, watch the door open, pause, and close again. Or maybe it was something else altogether. Whatever it was, we needed to figure out how to head Sam off before he walked himself to the store again.

Despite the danger of Sam's impromptu decision-making, I couldn't help but marvel at his ability to remember the location of Stefan's Market. It was as if he carried a map of Windsor inside his head. Sam had been to Stefan's only a few times, and it had been months since he last walked to the store with Mark or me. How many maps did he have like that in his head? I wondered whether any other four-year-old on the planet had such recall.

The questions tumbled in my mind as I joined Mark, Mom, and the boys in the minivan for our second try at a trip to the store.

Mercifully, Sam never walked himself to Stefan's Market, or anywhere else, ever again. Mom and Dad's house stayed quiet and calm most of the summer.

I signed Sam up for gymnastics class and swimming lessons through Windsor's parks and recreation program. That bit of schedule brought a comforting routine to each day. Sam learned to somersault on the giant tumbling mats. Some mornings started so cool and dry that swimming lessons made Sam's lips blue, in addition to pickling his fingertips. But as the lazy days wore on, the afternoons got hot enough that swimming became the best way to cool down.

Windsor removed the old city pool from Fifth Street's north end—where I had made tentative steps in healing from my eating disorder fifteen years before—and built a new pool next to the lush, green ball fields in the shadows of the old sugar mill. They took down the 0 Street sign and renamed it Chimney Park Drive. For Sam and the other four- and five-year-olds, lessons at Chimney Park pool consisted of hanging on the side wall, kicking, or putting faces into the water, blowing bubbles. The teacher also worked with the children, one by one, holding them afloat as they practiced moving their little bodies through the water—no resemblance to my first swimming lesson, when the instructor told parents that toddlers swim instinctively. Dad threw me in. I sank to the bottom. The lifeguard fished me out.

At Fifth and Main, the Rexall drugstore still had its old-fashioned soda fountain, so once in a while we walked to get an ice cream cone at the counter, especially if the boys asked for one.

Mom's friend Kitty came over once a week to work with Sam, playing simple games or with windup toys. She offered the kind of speech therapy and parent training we got from Nancy, only more. She taught me how to read research studies for new ideas to help Sam. I watched her use a few hand signs with Sam to great effect, especially the "pay attention" sign. I thought I might have to learn sign language, but she assured me that Sam's speech progress was good enough.

Michael started walking not long after we arrived. He was fifteen months old, so it was time. But I suspected he also wanted to keep up with his seven-year-old cousin, Ronnie, a more patient playmate than Sam.

Yet Michael and Sam had their moments, too. One night Sam opened up a toy doctor bag and Michael waited patiently as Sam took his temperature and measured his blood pressure. Chris, who bought the doctor bag for them, scrambled to capture the tender moment on her video camera.

Chris often thought of toys Sam would enjoy that I wouldn't have. One day she dusted off an old Simon Says music toy that

Ronnie had lost interest in. She invited Sam to play with her. Sam easily remembered the toy's challenging patterns of light and sound. He often played by himself, since the toy could call out to him, literally, all summer long.

Chris, Karen, and Teresa did a lot to bring the laughter back. They burst into giggles at some of the things Sam said, which helped Mark and me reconnect with the lighter side. Sam didn't mind the reaction at all. Sam's observation, "Grandpa, you have no hair, just a head," set off peals of sisterly laughter, much to Dad's chagrin. Decorum broke down at Mass when Sam rushed to the altar, pointing and warning us about the candles. "Fire is hot. Yep. See it? Right there? Fire is hot. Yep." Even the priest had to choke back laughter. Sam's perspective was like no other I'd ever known, and by accepting his new kind of normal, the rest of the world became a hilarious place.

Both boys loved Mom's garden. She pushed them gently on the swing set. They would sit on the lawn furniture next to her as she read books and poetry to them. She gave them little tours of her backyard oasis, pointing out flowers and offering strawberries for snacks. Dad announced when he was going to mow the grass so that Sam could fire up his toy lawn mower and follow along.

Mark forwent some of his practice time to clean up an old patio bike of Ronnie's so the three cousins could ride together. Ronnie showed Sam the secrets of riding through puddles when afternoon thunderclouds actually brought a little rain. Michael scooted on a tricycle as they all splashed, made wakes, and dragged tire tracks in and out of the gutters. Mark also helped Sam play simple ball games and took him to the park to swing harder and climb higher than he could at home.

From his patient cousin and brother, his taciturn grandfather, and his gentle grandmother, to his three loving, albeit giggly, aunts, Sam's interactions with everyone helped his social progress, too.

All summer, Mark and I took time to ride the tandem, or go out to dinner, or window-shop. Too many years had gone by since we could relax alone, confident the boys were well cared for, and simply enjoy each other's company.

We had suffered so much chaos and confusion. We weren't married long enough before Sam was born to have the emotional connective tissue the two of us needed to share the burden. I was stunned that our marriage survived the strain. But we managed to keep our fifteen-year friendship intact. For the rest of it, I thought perhaps the lay minister had summoned the Hawaiian gods as Mark and I held hands and declared our vows. We were still holding hands and the boys were tucked safely inside the circle.

But living with Sam came with an intrinsic lesson—start each day fresh, as if old hurts never happened. And loving Sam came with the most beautiful lesson of all—don't be afraid of your heart, because it will lead you straight into the light.

This second-chance summer had one more musical adventure for me, likely my last. I reached as far as I could before the busyness of our lives in California would return. Sometimes I listened to Aaron Copland's *Appalachian Spring* or *El Salón México* on headphones, to make sure my analysis was right. Sometimes I just listened to the sound of Mom's refrigerator humming and my pencil scratching. I got up before nearly everyone and worked for a few hours before the boys awoke. The rhythm of our days reminded me of Sam's newest favorite book—thanks to Mom—*The Napping House* and its lilting, cumulative rhymes.

"There is a house,
a napping house,
where everyone is sleeping."

Dad and Mark got up before me, before dawn even, and took turns milking cows at Larry and Rose's farm early in the morning and again in the evening. Larry and Rose commuted to Denver to stay close by their sixteen-year-old son, Jeremy, who needed chemotherapy treatments for bone cancer. Larry paid Dad and Mark about five dollars an hour for their help. That soon gave way to Dad and Mark calculating the cost of things by how many hours they would have to milk cows to pay for it. Yet, Larry and Rose's descending tragedy also reminded us just how fortunate we were that Sam was healthy and happy.

"And in that house . . . there is a child,
a dreaming child
on a snoring granny
on a cozy bed
 in a napping house,
where everyone is sleeping."

I planned to wake Sam at eight o'clock, since he needed to eat a good breakfast before his swimming lesson.
I heard a sound.

"Can it be? A wakeful flea . . ."

Sam was already up. I heard him scamper to the bathroom, signaling enough adventure for now in Aaron Copland's wide, open musical spaces. I wondered which one of Sam's maps would unfold today. Music gave me mine. When deep emotions threaten to overwhelm me, music opens a space for them, a place to live and breathe within me.

"... who thumps ...

who bumps ..."

Now Michael was up. I didn't like to roust him, but the moment he heard Sam moving around, he wanted to join the band, too.

I headed toward their bedroom.

"... in the napping house, where no one now is sleeping."

"Good morning, Michael! Good morning, Sam!" I said, pulling Michael from his crib.

Michael padded to the kitchen, where Mom was pulling out cereal, milk and bananas. She made cinnamon rolls the day before, using a favorite family recipe. Michael could have one for a mid-morning snack while we sat poolside and watched swim class.

Seeing Sam paddle around the pool, trying to swim as his instructor asked, I realized I was no longer afraid. My world hadn't become small again and it never would. Music wouldn't go away either. Even if I left my instrument behind, making fewer of those glorious living, breathing spaces for myself, I would be fine. Any time I listened, a musical map would unfold in my mind just the same.

My favorite spaces come at the end of a big work. The orchestra's inner voices rise up through the quieting waves and gently turn down the covers on the last few notes. With the viola's tender down bow, I can feel the heartbeat of it all.

Maybe Dr. Copeland called it, and in ten or twelve years, Sam would be all right. Getting him there was something else altogether, but I didn't need any more rehearsal.

I picked up his beach towel. I was ready. I felt it in my marrow as I held my hand out to his.

"Come on, Sam! Time to go!"

EPILOGUE

DURING OUR FIRST WEEKS back in Sacramento in the fall of 1992, we sought out many of the sort of services for Sam, both from the school and in the community, that resembled the impressive programs we saw in Syracuse.

Sam attended kindergarten in the morning. The special education teacher and one of the kindergarten teachers combined their students and curriculum into one room with a lot of help from the teachers' aides. I liked to think that guests visiting the classroom wouldn't be able to tell, at first blush, which kids were special, just like I couldn't tell the difference among the students in the integrated classrooms in Syracuse.

In the afternoon, Sam went to a Montessori school, where he spent a lot time around kids his own age. That helped his speech and social development as much as his schoolwork did. Mark and I still spent an hour or two each day working with Sam on small things we knew were important, such as taking turns playing games or learning to use a fork and knife.

Shortly before the holidays, I discovered that I was pregnant with our third child. A week later, the Sacramento Symphony declared bankruptcy, which derailed Mark's career. Because of proposed cuts in the state budget, we were also afraid my new

"I'm caring for my sister Paige."

job with the California Arts Council would be eliminated with a sweep of the governor's pen.

We decided to move to Texas, hoping for better career opportunities. Old friends from North Texas State, now the University of North Texas, helped us make the leap. We sold our house in California, and rented a small house in the tiny town of Argyle, about ten miles south of Denton. Eventually, we were able to buy ten acres and build our own home in the hopes that the children would enjoy opportunities afforded by life on a farm.

We had braced ourselves for fewer social services and less progressive schools than New York, or even California, especially after we learned that many Texas schools still paddled children as a form of discipline. But Argyle's teachers had big hearts and enormous energy. During the first few weeks at Argyle Elementary, for example, Sam had trouble staying focused on his work through the sound of the school bells. Principal Gaye Pittman simply turned them all off. She told the teachers that, until further notice, they needed to keep track of the time themselves. I had been responsible for so much of Sam's education for so long, it felt a little foreign to just sit back and let the teachers do their job. I enjoyed just being Sam's mom.

Watching Sam's progress over the last dozen years has been one of the great joys of my life. He graduated from high school with the rest of his class. He's a big fan of Harry Potter and John R. Erickson's *Hank the Cowdog* misadventures. With the help of a Texas Rehabilitative Services job coach, he got his first part-time job as a courtesy clerk at Albertsons. He takes several classes each semester at North Central Texas College in Corinth with the help of advisors and counselors in the access programs. And he's learning how to drive.

In high school, Sam took four years of Spanish, science and math, and was on the honor roll more often than not. He has struggled with some of his college studies. Yet he is undeterred. Sam is steadfast and determined to live an independent life. I'm confident he will achieve his goal. Read his "Senior Scrapbook" on the next page to see if you agree.

My Life Right Now

by Sam Wolfe

November 2005

THIS SUMMER, MY MOM WON FIRST PRIZE on a book about me when I was very young. The book is getting published in a year or two. The newspaper already reported her results and her pictures with me in the newspaper. I now have to write about my life right now until January 2006. When I write this story, the book will be able to get published. When the book gets published, my mom will keep her story and so will I. My grandparents and many other relatives in my family will even keep this story when it gets published.

On June 18, 2005, I attended the Denton County Fruit, Vegetable, Herb, and Flower Show in Denton, Texas, that took place near the Denton Area Teachers Credit Union. This is an event where people compete by showing fruits, vegetables, herbs, and flowers in a certain style. I got Grand Champion for a sunflower arrangement and Reserve Champion for some green beans. My sister, Paige, got Reserve Champion for her dill. I made thirty dollars for the sunflower arrangement and twenty

"Mom made 250 buttons out of my class picture."

dollars for the green beans. (I heard a rumor this was reported in another newspaper, before my mom won her prize for the book about me, so I was already famous.)

Some of my other Argyle 4-H club members attended this show. So, this was probably an event not only for a lot of experienced gardeners, but also for some of the Denton County 4-H clubs.

I also have horseback riding on Wednesday from six o'clock to seven o'clock at Riding Unlimited in Ponder. I am now learning about showmanship, equitation, and trail riding. We usually attend Chisholm Challenge in Fort Worth and State Special Olympics in Waco. Chisholm Challenge takes place in January before the Fort Worth Stock Show and Rodeo, and State Special Olympics takes place in May. Both events last for about two days. I have attended Chisholm Challenge and State Special

Olympics for two years in a row. These events normally have equitation, trail, showmanship, and sometimes a relay race. They do two events on the first day and another event, plus the horse races, on the second day. Before I go to State Special Olympics, I have to attend the regional Special Olympics that takes place in April. It is normally held where I go for horseback riding in Ponder, and has the same events, but it takes place only for one day.

I have been in 4-H since my freshman year here and this is my fourth year. Our club usually attends county and district food shows, works community service, and shows projects at the Denton County Livestock Association Youth Fair. Our club has meetings on the first Tuesday of each month.

The county food show takes place in the month that usually comes before the month of the district food show in the county extension office building in Denton. The district food show itself takes place at the student center at Texas A & M in Commerce.

My community service usually includes making pies for the Argyle Community Thanksgiving Dinner and Christmas place-mats for Meals on Wheels. The DCLA Fair takes place in March at the North Texas State Fairgrounds in Denton where people show pigs, cows, sheep, goats, and chickens, as well as plants. The DCLA Fair is like the State Fair of Texas, except that the State Fair takes place in October at the fairgrounds in Dallas. People also compete in these fairs to win money like at the Denton County Fruit, Vegetable, Herb, and Flower Show.

I also like to go out with my friends on weekends to see a movie, to eat at a restaurant, and to do other things. I usually talk to them about that between classes at school, or during class free time. Sometimes, I have to call them at night, especially if I don't see them between classes or they get too busy to talk to at school.

Almost every time that I call my friends, I have to leave them a message, even at the latest appropriate time I call them, for some reason (i.e., they are too busy to answer the phone. Some phone lines are programmed to automatically prompt you to leave a message if they're in use, instead of giving you a busy signal. Or they possibly have their phone line shut down at night).

I usually have to set up the outing at the beginning or the middle of the week so my friends know which day and what time on the weekend to either meet me, or where I want to meet them, or to swing by my house to pick me up and take me out. I usually ask them to pick me up because it's more accurate. Sometimes, if you ask them to meet you where you want to go, they don't show up, even if they tell you they would. So, doing this is risky, if your family has to take you where you want to go.

You can get in trouble if your family has to take you out to meet your friends, but they suddenly don't show up at any time. If your friends can only meet you at your destination, you *must* ask one of your buddies to pick you up.

On the night of the homecoming dance, I went to the Olive Garden in Denton with the special education class. After dinner, we went to the dance. I didn't have a dance partner, like I did when Maggie and I went to the junior-senior prom, but I did enjoy the dance a little bit.

During the 4-H Gold Star Banquet, the Denton County Judge presented me with the Brave Heart Scholarship Award, which made me feel like I was one of the bravest 4-H members.

General Autism Information

Autism Society of America, *www.autism-society.org*

We've been to the annual conferences that this organization and its affiliates sponsor, noting that they are the flagship for autism information and advocacy in the United States They have information for individuals with autism, parents, teachers, and others in the helping professions. At various times, we've also tapped into the resources to be had by local chapters, which sponsor their own activities in support of their communities. The American Psychiatric Association's *Diagnostic and Statistical Manual of Mental Disorders* officially describes the diagnostic criteria for autism and related disorders, but here is the ASA's definition of autism:

> Autism is a complex developmental disability that typically appears during the first three years of life and is the result of a neurological disorder that affects the normal functioning of the brain, impacting development in the areas of social interaction and communication skills. Both children and adults with autism typically show difficulties in verbal and nonverbal communication, social interactions, and leisure or play

activities. One should keep in mind, however, that autism is a spectrum disorder and it affects each individual differently and at varying degrees. . . .

Autism is one of five disorders that falls under the umbrella of Pervasive Developmental Disorders (PDD), a category of neurological disorders characterized by "severe and pervasive impairment in several areas of development." The five disorders under PDD are:

- Autistic Disorder
- Asperger's Disorder
- Childhood Disintegrative Disorder (CDD)
- Rett's Disorder
- Pervasive Developmental Disorder-Not Otherwise Specified (PDD-NOS)

American Speech-Language-Hearing Association, *www.asha.org*

We knew Sam was in trouble around age two because he spoke so little. We soon learned the difference between receptive language (hearing and understanding) and expressive language (talking). While Sam's speech didn't develop at a normal pace, it did seem to follow the pattern of normal development. We wanted to recognize new skills in hearing and understanding when they emerged so we could encourage Sam to express himself when the opportunities came up in our everyday interactions. Weekly sessions with the speech pathologist were helpful for him, but we found it important that we became familiar with the normal development patterns ourselves. The association's Web site includes valuable information for parents to help foster speech development. Here are the stages of speech and language development for babies, toddlers and preschoolers within their typical time frame:

Birth to One Year

Birth–3 Months

Hearing and Understanding

- Startles to loud sounds.
- Quiets or smiles when spoken to.
- Seems to recognize your voice and quiets if crying.
- Increases or decreases sucking behavior in response to sound.

Talking

- Makes pleasure sounds (cooing, gooing).
- Cries differently for different needs.
- Smiles when sees you.

4–6 Months

Hearing and Understanding

- Moves eyes in direction of sounds.
- Responds to changes in tone of your voice.
- Notices toys that make sounds.
- Pays attention to music.

Talking

- Babbling sounds more speech-like with many different sounds, including *p*, *b* and *m*.
- Vocalizes excitement and displeasure.
- Makes gurgling sounds when left alone and when playing with you.

7 Months–1 Year

Hearing and Understanding

- Enjoys games like peekaboo and pat-a-cake.
- Turns and looks in direction of sounds.
- Listens when spoken to.
- Recognizes words for common items like "cup," "shoe," "juice."
- Begins to respond to requests (e.g., "Come here," "Want more?").

Talking

- Babbling has both long and short groups of sounds, such as "tata upup bibibibi."
- Uses speech or non-crying sounds to get and keep attention.
- Imitates different speech sounds.
- Has one or two words (bye-bye, dada, mama) although they may not be clear.

One to Two Years

Hearing and Understanding

- Points to a few body parts when asked.
- Follows simple commands and understands simple questions ("Roll the ball," "Kiss the baby," "Where's your shoe?").
- Listens to simple stories, songs, and rhymes.
- Points to pictures in a book when named.

Talking

- Says more words every month.
- Uses some one- to two-word questions ("Where kitty?" "Go bye-bye?" "What's that?").
- Puts two words together ("more cookie," "no juice," "mommy book").
- Uses many different consonant sounds at the beginning of words.

Two to Three Years

Hearing and Understanding

- Understands differences in meaning ("go-stop," "in-on," "big-little," "up-down").
- Follows two requests ("Get the book and put it on the table").

Talking

- Has a word for almost everything.
- Uses two- to three-word "sentences" to talk about and ask for things.
- Speech is understood by familiar listeners most of the time.
- Often asks for or directs attention to objects by naming them.

Three to Four Years

Hearing and Understanding

- Hears you when call from another room.

- Hears television or radio at the same loudness level as other family members.
- Understands simple "wh" (who, what, where, why) questions.

Talking
- Talks about activities at school or at friends' homes.
- People outside family usually understand child's speech.
- Uses a lot of sentences that have four or more words.
- Usually talks easily without repeating syllables or words.

Four to Five Years

Hearing and Understanding
- Pays attention to a short story and answers simple questions about it.
- Hears and understands most of what is said at home and in school.

Talking
- Voice sounds clear like other children's.
- Uses sentences that give lots of details (e.g., "I like to read my books").
- Tells stories that stick to topic.
- Communicates easily with other children and adults.
- Says most sounds correctly except perhaps certain ones like *l, s, r, v, z, ch, sh, th*.
- Uses the same grammar as the rest of the family.

Some Autism Resources

Autism Autobiographies

Barron, Judy, and Sean Barron. *There's a Boy in Here*. Arlington, Tex.: Future Horizons, 2002. First published, New York: Simon & Schuster, 1992.

In this memoir, the mother and son describe situations side by side. I found the parallel vignettes bittersweet, but helpful in broadening my perspective. For example, Judy can't understand why Sean always has a temper tantrum when a waiter brings him water with ice. But Sean can't understand why waiters keep violating his preference for water without ice. (Sam doesn't like ice in his water either. It's too cold and causes the water to splash out when drinking.)

Grandin, Temple. *Animals in Translation: Using the Mysteries of Autism to Decode Animal Behavior*. New York: Scribner, 2005.

Temple wrote three books. This one focuses on her passion: the humane treatment of animals. She offers extraordinary, even revolutionary, insight into emotions and social learning; moreover, she puts operant conditioning in proper perspective.

———. *Emergence: Labeled Autistic*. New York: Warner Books, 1986.

Since this is her childhood memoir, she has insight into how children with autism think.

———. *Thinking in Pictures: And Other Reports from My Life with Autism.* New York: Vintage Books, 1995.

This book recalls fewer childhood experiences than *Emergence* does, but Temple tell us more about how she perceives the world and works her way through it. This book also helped me broaden my perspective.

Williams, Donna. *Nobody Nowhere.* New York: Times Books, 1992.

Donna relays other challenges besides having autism, including a mother who abused her. I found her book hard to read for its stream of consciousness, but valuable in understanding the adult perspective.

Parenting Resources

The Beach Center on Disability, *www.beachcenter.org*

Based at the University of Kansas, the center offers a number of resources on its Web site and call center. I found the parent-to-parent links the most helpful in finding older, more seasoned parents who had both reliable information and solid emotional support.

Frith, Uta. *Autism: Explaining the Enigma.* 2nd ed. Malden, Mass.: Blackwell, 2003. First published, Oxford, U.K.: Blackwell, 1989.

I enjoyed Frith's speculations over historic figures who might have had autism, which wasn't formally described until the 1940s. As a parent, I found the case descriptions of real human beings drew a picture of autism far less abstract than the official lists of general characteristics. Frith's book is now available in an expanded, updated second edition.

Harris, Sandra L., and Beth A. Glasberg. *Siblings of Children with Autism: A Guide for Families.* 2nd ed. Bethesda, Md.: Woodbine House, 2003.

Also in its second edition, this is one book I wish had been out when the kids were younger. However, we took part in a psychology study of siblings and children with autism. The researchers showed us how the boys could play together, and thus have a better relationship. Board games and other play that had some structure worked best for us. Sam couldn't do much pretend play with Michael. Of course, after video games came to our house, the boys were home free, though we still have a family game night from time to time.

Powers, Michael D., ed. *Children with Autism: A Parents' Guide*. 2nd ed. Bethesda, Md.: Woodbine House, 2000.

Now in its second edition, this reference guide is on its way to becoming a classic. I learned a lot about the special education system from this book and how to be an effective advocate for Sam.

Rolfe, Randy. *You Can Postpone Anything but Love*. New York: Warner Books, 1990.

Almost a treatise on the life cycle of human love, this book is dense and a little hard to read, but I found it well researched and persuasive. Rolfe underscores that we all come into the world as loving beings and that layers of loving interaction sustain love's vibrancy.

Health Resources

Ayres, A. Jean. *Sensory Integration and the Child*. 2nd ed. Los Angeles: Western Psychological Services, 2004. First published 1979.

Ayres draws on extensive clinical experience to develop her sensory integration theory. It's a seminal work for occupational therapy, as she walks through sensory dysfunction in meaningful ways. Addressing the therapeutic community, the first edition was a hard read for me, but it still helped sort through some of the odd things that Sam did—not only among five senses, but his vestibular system of movement and balance and his proprioceptive system, or awareness of his body in space. The publisher's second edition, which marks the book's twenty-fifth anniversary, was created to meet the continuing demand made by lay readers.

Centers for Disease Control and Prevention Web site, Act Early page, *www.cdc.gov/ncbddd/autism/actearly*

The CDC campaigned to alert family practitioners and pediatricians to the need to diagnose early. The Web site links to information about, and encourages doctors to take the time for, developmental screenings.

Checklist for Autism in Toddlers (CHAT)

This screening instrument for children eighteen months old was first described in a paper by Simon Baron-Cohen et al. published in the *Journal of the Royal Society of Medicine* 93, no. 10 (October 2000): 521–525. See a reprint and other tests at *www.autismresearchcentre. com/tests/default.asp*. Researchers have been refining the checklist, which has a U.S. version, the M-CHAT, and a Chinese version, the CHAT-23.

Journal of Autism and Developmental Disorders. Published since 1993, 1997–present are online at *www.springeronline.com*.

This journal can be a resource for doctors and allied health professionals as well as teachers and parents. Its original research papers cover behavioral, biological, educational, and community aspects of autism. One of Sam's speech therapists encouraged us to read autism research, telling us to simply skip past the literature review and methodology, which can be difficult for the lay reader, and go right to discussion and results. Those sections often had new, useful insights. For example, we learned how to use video modeling to teach some social skills by reading the research studies on the technique for ourselves.

National Institutes of Health Studies to Advance Autism Research and Treatment (STAART) Network, *www.nimh.nih.gov/autismiacc/ staart.cfm*

This research network, which began in 2000, includes studies identifying factors that distinguish children with autism from those without as early as eighteen to twenty-four months.

North American Riding for the Handicapped Association, P.O. Box 33150, Denver, Colo. 80233, *www.narha.org*

Sam has been in a NARHA-certified therapeutic horseback-riding program since he was five years old. Horseback riding provides stimulation that develops the trunk and core muscles that many kids with autism don't seem to develop normally. In addition, horseback riding reinforces a social relationship between the rider and the animal; the better a horseman Sam becomes, the better his ride. Some riders benefit from one-on-one lessons led by a physical therapist trained in hippotherapy, but other riders get enough benefit from small recreational classes led by experienced trainers. NARHA is a referral and certifying agency that helps establish and maintain ethical standards of professionalism and safety. Programs accredited by NARHA have submitted to outside review of their programs and operations.

Southpaw Enterprises, *www.southpawenterprises.com*

This company sells equipment for sensory integration activities, such as swings, mats, and ball pits. We adapted some of their mounting hardware to our Rainbow Play Systems swing set so that Sam could swing on both net and tire swings at home. We also bought a ball pit.

Educational Resources

Farrow, Elvira, and Carol Hill. *Montessori on a Limited Budget: A Manual for the Amateur Craftsman.* Ithaca, N.Y.: Montessori Workshop, 1975.

This book is full of simple projects for things you can make or build to help your child, and they are just as fun for children without autism.

Future Horizons, *www.futurehorizons-autism.com*

Founded by the father of a young man with autism, this publishing company specializes in educational books and guides on many topics in autism. They often hold conferences that help bring the authors of the material together with parents, teachers, and people with autism.

Inclusion, *www.inclusion.com*

Our visit to the preschool in Syracuse opened our eyes to the power of inclusion for kids with autism. Over the year, Sam benefited from being held to the same academic standards as the rest of the kids. But it was a challenge. Teachers and administrators, while easy to convince of the value of inclusive education in principle, didn't always have the skills to pull it off. Sadly, a few lacked the generous heart needed for success, too. At those times, we were happy for his schoolmates, who sometimes did better than the adults at helping Sam adapt. He picked up more social understanding by learning to get along with them, too.

Lekotek, *www.lekotek.org*

Maria Montessori was first to say that play is a child's work. Lekotek is an international network of toy libraries, adaptive computer devices, and trained therapists who help children with disabilities develop through play. Services we received from a Lekotek leader helped us realize that Sam got plenty of work done during his play-time, too. Our leader had a gift for finding toys that Sam responded to, even though much of her training was toward adapting toys for physical disabilities. I observed her closely and learned what to look for at the toy store. Many Lekotek chapters have family play sessions and toy lending libraries.

Montessori, Maria. *The Absorbent Mind*. New York: Holt, 1995. First published, New York: Holt, Rinehart & Winston, 1967.

Dispatched to teach the children living in the slums of Rome, Maria Montessori was far ahead of her time in observing and describing the way children learn, "a child's work," as she called it. Children are ready to soak up all they can through their five senses. I found it dense, but it helped me become a careful observer of Sam's readiness for different things to learn, whether it was letters or numbers or other concepts. He was just as spongelike as other kids when he had the right materials at the right time.

————. *The Montessori Method*. New York: Schocken Books, 1964.

In this book, she describes the science behind the learning activities that she designed. The most important idea I picked up from this book was the idea of toys that teach, often designed so that a child can readily see any errors and fix them. Sam always did better with learning activities that had a good structure or routine to them.

Counseling Resources

Circle of Friends, *www.inclusion.com/circlesoffriends.html*

Circle of Friends helps not only the child with the disability make friends but helps other children overcome their fear of interacting with children who are different from themselves. While this publish-ing company has a compendium of resources to support everyone in learning and living together, we were lucky in that Sam's elementary school counselor developed a program around it. I asked Michael Ball, Sam's counselor, how he came about his program, which has about twelve circles around kids who have difficulty making friends, and he offered this explanation:

> At my annual counselor's conference in Austin, I heard a presenter speak about how each one of us has circles around us. The first circle we have is our family; the second circle, close friends; third circle, groups of friends (teams, scouts, church, etc.); fourth, mere acquaintances (classmates, people we know their name and face, but not much else); and fifth, paid professionals (doctors, dentists, barbers, etc.). It is the second circle that is often the one that is the hardest for some people to develop, especially those with some type of disability that interferes with that.
>
> I looked for books and materials. I found a few things called "Circle of Friends," but as I worked with different kids, I began to realize quickly how different every child is and how there couldn't be that perfect curriculum. I think that it is about finding activities that the child with the disability can have some success with and that the rest of the group will enjoy to some extent. I have realized that Circle usually works best when I provide the activity and then let things unfold. I facilitate my groups by helping the kids solve problems and by providing them information about the nature of each disability.

"Social Stories." Gray Center for Social Learning and Understanding, *www.thegraycenter.org*

I attended one of Carol Gray's lectures and learned how kids with autism miss social cues. Then she explained how, once those cues are described, kids with autism can figure out the correct social response. Social Stories are the best of several techniques that she developed to explain these cues. We bought a sample collection of stories to get started. My favorite was a one-page story explaining how to hug. "Put your arms around someone and squeeze gently."